Social Media Marketing

Secret Step-by-Step Strategies for Marketing and Advertising Your Business to Millions on Facebook, Instagram, YouTube and Twitter, While Branding Yourself or Your Business as an Influencer in 2019 and Beyond

By Gary Clyne

Table of Contents

Introduction

Social Media Marketing is currently the most powerful tool that can help businesses (whether small or not) to reach customers and prospects. But with over 88 percent of all the companies marketing their businesses on at least one social media platform, you can see how easy can be for your brand to get lost in all that noise.

In order for your business social media pages to gain more organic exposure, reach to engaged brand advocates, and even drive more sales and leads, you will need a concise marketing strategy to rise to the top. Luckily for you, this book offers just that.

Peeling through the layers of the most popular social media platforms to get to the core of what makes an online marketing strategy successful, this book will teach you just how to promote your brand on social media.

Whether you are already active on social media or have never had a Facebook account, this book will guide your social media marketing plan every step of the way – from the creation of your account and optimizing your profile, through posting content that your audience will want to engage with, and all the way to advertising and promoting your brand for more traffic and followers.

Covering Facebook, YouTube, Instagram, Twitter, LinkedIn, and Pinterest, this guide will show you that social media marketing can bring success to your business, despite the fierce competition.

A strong social media presence is something your business cannot afford to miss out on. Read on to see how to create a killer social media marketing plan that will instantly drive thousands of followers to your profile.

The Importance of Social Media

Unless you have been living under a rock, chances are, you are more than familiar with the term *social media*. In fact, you probably have an active account on at least one of the popular social media platforms. For the sake of your time, I will not go into defining social media or bore you with its early rise. Instead, let's look at why is that social media is so important and how to take advantage of its popularity.

Easy and convenient connecting with friends and family aside, social media offers many other advantages that people in the past couldn't enjoy. From getting to know people from all over the world, to staying updated with the latest news, sharing your opinion, and discovering new things, products, and services, social media has become an inevitable part of the modern society of today.

Growing with an insanely fast pace, the social networks are now one of the fastest growing industries in the world. It is no doubt that many businesses have taken advantage of the activity on social media and managed to increase their conversion.

If you think of social media as nothing but a trend that is doomed to fade away, you cannot be more wrong. With more and more people joining every day and using the social media platforms efficiently for various purposes, it is safe to say that the social media industry is definitely at its peak and will only grow bigger in the years to come.

If you want for your business to evolve, then forget about newspapers or TV ads, because right now, social media is the ticket for expanding your company.

Statistics Don't Lie

If I still haven't managed to convince you that marketing your business on the most popular social media platforms is the best business strategy for your product/service today, then perhaps these statistics will cast some light and help you realize that presenting your business on social media is the best way to reach your target audience.

As of 2019, there are 7.7 billion people in the world today. It is interesting to know that 4.2 billion of these people are internet users, but what's even more fascinating is the fact that more than 2.7 billion of the internet users are active on social media. That means that over 64% of the people that surf the internet spend some efficient time on social media. In fact, according to many studies done in the past few years, the average time that people - spend on social media is nearly 2 hours, or more precisely, 117 minutes. No wonder why most of the small businesses that are active on social media post daily. Since statistics also say that there is a new social media user practically every 10 seconds, it is pretty obvious why signing up your business for some social media activity can turn out to be highly profitable.

Read on to see what social media marketing can throw your way as well as to find out how to successfully jumpstart the whole process.

Why My Business Needs Social Media?

At this point, not being present on social media is like flipping through a telephone book to find the number of your hairdresser. Or still owning a Nokia 3310. And while there is nothing wrong with using a two-decade-old cell phone model or keeping it old-school with hand-written telephone books, one thing is certain – those people miss out on the perks of today's technology. And that's perfectly fine. If you are just a guy who has a no-modern-technology principle, that is. But if you are a business that is looking for a way to increase the conversion and reap as many benefits as possible, then being present online is a must.

For many people social media is the internet, so they spend their hours scrolling down their social media platforms. Why? Because there is no reason to leave, actually. From chatting with people, to being up-to-date with news and finding and buying products and services, the social networks literally have it all. If you want your business to be successful, then having a strong social media presence is of great essence.

If your business is still not active on social media, then that is definitely the missing link that can strengthen the connection between your product/service and your customers. Still not sure whether it is worth the time and effort? Here are the benefits of being present on the social networks:

Web Traffic

Marketing your business on social media is a crucial part for your web traffic:

Posting on Social Media Drives Your Targeted Audience

Of course you want your business to be the first thing people will see when surfing the internet for similar products/services. But is that really possible if you are not active online? Posting regularly on social media will help you take domination over the first search page which will, in turn, increase your profits.

These social media posts are extremely valuable for increasing web traffic. For instance, think about what happens when you update your website. It surely takes a while for it to get traction with the search engines, right? That means that the number of customers that will be aware of your new content will be limited. Posting on social media will help your potential customers find your new content easily and then be re-directed to your website. This means that you don't have to wait for a customer to click on your website to find out your updates. Social media allows you to reach potential customers even if they are not looking to buy at that exact moment,

Social Media Posts Boosts the SEO

Search engine optimization is of great importance for your online presence and overall business. Don't be fooled that this is not that important. SEO experts know which sites have constant traffic and which sits lonely and forgotten. A great content strategy can obviously skyrocket your search rankings, however, social media posts also have the power to drive more traffic to your site. By re-sharing popular content you can easily optimize your page and lure existing and potential customers to take a peek. The boosted traffic will then lead to inbound clicks and will have a significant impact on your prominence in Google rankings.

Quoting Can Make You More Reachable

Sometimes, a simple quote can throw more traffic your way. Whether you have used a PR tool such as HARO to find experts for your site or you simply want to quote an expert with a strong influence on social media, this can surely help your business. Chances are, by quoting (and tagging!) an expert in your tweet or Facebook post, that person will most likely share or retweet your post which will help you reach potential customers from their list of followers and increase your site's traffic.

Connecting with Customers

Being the bridge that can connect the gap between you and your customers, social media is definitely the shortcut you need to take in order to reach your audience the fastest way possible.

Reaching Customers

Social media is perhaps the only tool that can help you reach customers from all age groups at once. These networks are not just for teenagers searching for entertainment. The social media platforms are actively used by more than 2.7 billion people, so it is safe to say that whatever your target audience is, your potential customers are spending some efficient time on social media already. In fact, a study has actually found that 37% of all the Americans over 65 years of age are social media users.

Whether you want to reach young adults, housewives, or retirees, social media is the best place to introduce your product/service to them.

Besides, advertising on social media allows targeting and retargeting your audience which can play a crucial role in your marketing strategy. For instance, the ads on Facebook can be filtered around the needs of your customers and target only the age, location, industry, etc. of the audience that you are trying to reach.

Learning about Your Target Audience

Perhaps the biggest reason why social media marketing is so game-changing for businesses is the fact that these networks actually allow you to have a real interaction with your existing and potential customers. This creates an incredible opportunity to peek inside your audience's lives and learn about the customer behaviors first-hand. By reading posts and tweets, you can easily find the answers to the questions that every business is mostly concerned with:

- What product/services do people want to buy and why?

- What kind of websites do people mostly visit?

- What are the biggest hobbies nowadays and how can my product/service help?

- What types of posts do people share the most?

Finding the answers to these questions will help you understand your customers and allow you to write compelling posts and tweets that people will find appealing. By retweeting and sharing, you will not only increase the traffic and eventually profits, but also pinpoint what are the disappointments of the customers and how to refine your product/service in order to increase conversion.

Getting Noticed Easily

Imagine that you are hosting an event. A decent promotion is kind of required, right? What best way to do it than to have an active social media presence? Social media platforms will help you spread the word which will not only bring more guests, but can also throw a few big perks your way such as finding donors that are eager to participate.

Improving Your Brand's Image

Marketing your product/service on social media can help you thrive as a company, increase the exposure of your brand, and make its image recognizable and trustworthy.

The Best Customer Service Tool

Building a great image for your brand starts with keeping your customers happy and content. Many studies have shown that customers mostly reward those companies that take the time to quickly respond to their inquiries. But quickly responding to complaints isn't what it used to be. If there is a customer request pending, they are expecting for the issue to be solved right away.

Social media helps you offer customer service that is quick, helpful, and proactive, and gives you the opportunity to reach and help your customers before they get the chance to call your call center.

This little trick just saved British Telecom over 2 million pounds in customer service costs, so just let that sink in for a second.

Building Up the Loyalty of Your Brand

This is actually pretty self-explanatory, but it would be remiss not to mention it. By taking the time to engage with your customers actively and provide them with beneficial info, help with inquiries, and keep them entertained without asking a thing in return, your brand's loyalty is actually enhanced.

The right social media presence can bring value to the customers and show them that you are not looking to empty their pockets, but that you actually care whether they are satisfied with your product/service or not.

Getting Started With Social Media Marketing

Posting family pictures and restaurant check-ins, does not actually make you a social media guru. Even if you have an active account that you use regularly, there are a lot more angles that need to be considered when looking to use social networks as a strong marketing tool. You need to stop looking at social media as a user, but as someone who is trying to reach all users.

Did you know that Instagram has its highest traffic between 9 and 11 am? Or that you can actually communicate on Twitter in six different ways? Do not skip this chapter thinking you are expert on social media, but read on to see how you can scratch the surface and find the best way to start your social media marketing.

Making Your Social Media Marketing Plan

In order to slay the competition and help your business thrive on social media, good planning ahead is indeed required. Your approach to social media marketing must take into consideration the real picture of the market, the needs of your target audience, but also the wants and needs of your business. If you don't know where to start and how to craft your ideal strategy, these steps will most likely help you design a decent plan:

#1: Check Your Social Media Presence

If you are not just starting out, then chances are your business is already present on some of the social media platforms. Before you create a strategy and head somewhere, take a good look at your networks and review where you are currently standing:

- Which platforms are you present on?

- Are your profiles optimized?

- Is some network bringing you value already?

- What do your profiles look like when compared to the competition?

If you are not present on social media, the next chapters will help you create killer accounts. But before you do that, peek into the competitors' profiles to see what they are currently offering.

#2: Define Your Ideal Customer

Someone said that the main goal of marketing is to know exactly what your customers need in order for the product to practically sells itself. Keep that in mind when thinking about your ideal customers. You will need to get pretty specific if you want to avoid marketing to the wrong kind of audience.

Before you actually start marketing, you will need to know exactly who your customer is. Here is a great example of how your customers should be defined: *A stay-at-home mom between 25 and 40 years of age who lives in the United States, lives in a house in the suburbs, primarily uses Instagram and has a thing for crafting activities.*

To define the buyer persona that your product/service is created for, answer the following questions:

- Age

- Location

- Job Title and Income

- Interests

- Pain Points (that can be solved by the usage of your product/service)

- Most Used Social Network

#3: Have a Social Media Marketing Mission Line

This may seem silly to some, but having a mission statement can help you stay focused and keep your eye on the ball at all times. This is what will actually drive all of your actions, so make sure that you come up with a good one. A great mission line should explain what your primary goal is, and what you are hoping to get out of social media marketing.

For instance, a good social media marketing mission statement should say: *"To use the social media platforms to help people learn about healthy eating, offer healthy and nutritious free recipes, and promote my new books."* Of course, this is just an example. Your mission statement can be whatever you are trying to achieve through marketing. The main point is to make sure that all of your posts and tweets align with that statement. If you post randomly and without any guiding goal, your marketing strategy will be doomed to fail.

#4: Decide on Your Metrics

For your social media marketing to be successful, you will have to have a decent measuring strategy. If you don't measure your posts the right way, you will fail to improve your marketing, and may even end up losing customers. That's why a good measuring plan is important.

How will you decide whether your social media marketing strategies are successful? What will the key success metrics be? What is important to you? Here are some metrics that can help you whether you are marketing your products/servicer the right way:

- Total Shares

- Conversion Rate

- Total Mentions of Your Brand

- Time Spent on Your Website

- Reach

- Sentiment

#5: Think About Investing in Social Media Management

If you are planning on marketing on various platforms and be super-active on social media in order to reap the benefits, then chances are that you will be crunched for time. That means that you might not be able to measure and track the progress of your social media marketing strategies. In order for you to stay up-to-date with the things that your customers like the most (as well as what they don't appreciate) so you can improve and provide more value, you need to have a social media management tool to increase your productivity.

Depending on your needs, there are various tools to choose from. https://hootsuite.com/, https://sproutsocial.com/ and https://buffer.com/ offer some great options. Choose the right pricing and plan your investment in these tools accordingly.

The Best 5 Social Media Marketing Strategies to Increase Productivity

Whether you call them strategies, habits, or just a way of marketing on social media, there are some things that you need to take care of in order to dust off your lonely business social channel. Or develop a successful routine, in case your business is new to the social media world, that is.

Strategy #1: Set Your Scheme and Stick to It

If you do not have a thought out strategy, your posts and tweets will probably just go unnoticed. Besides your objectives, which should already be firmly set, you also need to have a good course of action about how you will actually get to your primarily goal.

Choosing what and when to post is a good example of an organized scheme. You should have a set limit of how many posts you think about publishing daily. Decide on your strategy, and stick to it. Of course, you will adjust this on the go, but the most important thing is to keep yourself organized and punctual.

Scheduling posts is, obviously, just one example. In the following chapters you will come across many schemes for successful social media marketing that you should take advantage of.

Strategy #2: Post Regularly and Be Consistent

In order to keep your customers interested in your product or service, you will have to have a good posting strategy. Providing regular content is a great marketing strategy as it helps your customers stay updated, plus it shows that you are always looking for ways to improve and provide even more value. However, as important as regular content is, it will be pretty useless if you do not have a consistent approach.

The best way to provide regular content and to maintain its consistency is if you know exactly what your audience is looking for. Do your homework well before hitting the "share" button.

Strategy #3: Approach Your Social Media Channels Differently

Despite the fact that you are marketing the same product/service, you need to keep in mind that you are actually doing it on different social media platforms. What does that mean? That means that you cannot simply copy and paste your posts. Why? Because different platforms usually means different audience. Many of Instagram followers will not be LinkedIn users and vice versa.

For instance, LinkedIn is more business-oriented and its content is a bit more serious and educational than, for example, Instagram, which it has users who are mostly looking for appealing and vivid visual posts.

Treat your social media channels as different entities and keep the post separated and, most importantly, unique. Even if you are looking to spread the same message, make sure you adjust it for the different types of audience.

Strategy #4: Stay Engaged

Engagement is all that social media is about. It is a process of keeping in touch, listening, and painting the picture that your audience actually want to see. Social media marketing is not marketing if you are not 100% engaged. And not only with your posts and shares, but with answering, retweeting, and responding to complaints, as well. Your customers need to know that you care about them, and if you are not engaged, well, your other strategies will also be pretty useless.

The best way to make the audience notice your engagement is to keep them involved at all times. Ask for their opinion, make questionnaires, come up with unique competitions, offer rewards, discounts, etc. Keeping your business connected to your customers is the secret behind every successful marketing strategy.

Strategy #5: Act like a Human

Social media is all about the human interaction, not pitches and logos. This can be somewhat tricky when you are just starting your social media marketing journey as most companies make their initial approach a hard selling point. Avoid putting off potential and existing customers with customer reviews, product introductions, and purchasing codes. Instead, make your approach as friendly as possible.

But do not implement this only in the beginning. Your business should find a way to always act like a person (to some degree, of course), not to approach customers as an entity.

Killer Content is the Key

Like any other marketing strategy, if your social media marketing doesn't have any returns, then you are investing the wrong way. And your investment on social media is the content you post.

Your customers expect you to bring value. If your posts are not valuable then it is pretty impossible to keep the audience engaged. After all, it is the content that drives traffic to your page. In order for your social media marketing to turn out beneficial, you will need to know exactly what types of content to share and why. And yes, there is more than one way of sharing.

User-Generated Content

The content that is produced by unpaid contributors is called user-generated content. This makes perfect sense if you think about it, since it is in our nature to try new products/services based on other people's recommendations in order to avoid making mistakes or disappointing ourselves. There are more chances that we will respond positively to a photo shared by a friend than a photo shared by a brand.

This type of content will not only bring authenticity to your brand, but it will also connect your company to your customers in a more human way.

GIFS

GIF is a very popular image type that supports both, static and animated images. This image type is especially attractive to younger population thanks to its interesting visual elements. Choosing to add GIFs to your page will give a message to your audience (whatever age group they belong to) that you follow recent trends and that you actually listen.

If you want to keep your customers captivated and stimulated visually, then adding GIFs is the right choice.

Infographics

If you have to discuss a more complex subject but don't want to bore your customers with heavy and dull reading, then graphics are the perfect decision. Properly designed graphics cannot only simplify a complicated topic, but will also attract the customer's eye, even if they are not really interested in the particular subject. Infographics are an extremely valuable tool for your social media marketing, so make sure to incorporate them whenever you get the chance.

Concept Visualization

Infographics are great and super effective, but only if you are not trying to tell a really long story. Otherwise, it is pretty hard to design them in a way that will cover enough info and keep the customer's attention. Another powerful tool for simplifying complex topics is concept visualization.

Concept visualization are all those graphs, charts, and visuals that are basically self-explanatory. Here, by illustrating a single idea you can present your story in a smaller, fun, and a much more absorbable way. Besides, they are more shareable than infographics which makes them perfect for your social media marketing.

Live Streaming

Live streaming is a great way to lure traffic into your page, but that is not the only reason. While you are streaming and gaining more views, you can also add additional info about your service or product and actually know that people are reading it. Besides, live streaming is also great for interacting with your customers through some Q&As and learning about what they want first hand.

Facebook

Assuming that you already know how big Facebook is, I will not try to convince you why you need to open a Facebook account. Besides, when you say it like that, *your business needs a Facebook page*, it sounds like a pretty obvious understatement. But I will give you a taste of the newest statistics and make you understand why having a decent marketing strategy on Facebook can be of huge importance for your overall business.

Although Facebook has been a big deal practically since the day it was invented, its marketing side now offers tools that we didn't think were even possible 10 years ago. From selling services via your chatbot and promoting your product in a 360-degree video, Facebook marketing is a standard that all businesses must meet.

The fact that Facebook has 2.27 billion active users, from which 1.49 billion use this platform actively on daily basis, is a pretty good reason why you should seriously invest in marketing your brand on

Facebook. When the average person spends 50 minutes per day on this platform, you can only imagine how huge of a marketplace this network can be.

And while it is true that Facebook is one crowded marketplace, not taking advantage of the tools that it offers can be a terrible mistake for your business. Being as huge as it is, the odds are, your competition is already out there, promoting their products on this platform. Sitting this out is simply not something that your business can afford. It may seem scary, but if done correctly and with just the right amount of effort, you too could have amazing returns. Let this chapter guide your way for a successful marketing journey.

Creating Your Facebook Page

First things first, in order to market on Facebook, you must have a Facebook page up and running. By doing that, you will be joining 60 million businesses from all over the world that are promoting their brands on this platform. It sounds intimidating, I know, but that's why this step is so important. Creating a killer page can really make a huge difference in the whole marketing process. Before you start posting quality content, you need to have a personalized page, first.

If you already have a personal account, then you probably know how this works. Pages for businesses are what profile pages are for people. People connect with people by 'adding' them as friends, and follow businesses by 'liking' their pages. Why am I mentioning this? If you, by any chance, decide to open a profile for your business instead of a page, Facebook may shut it down permanently since it's against their rules.

To start this process, go to https://www.facebook.com/pages/creation/. There, you will see two different categories to choose from:

1. Business or Brand

2. Community or Public Figure

Assuming you are a business, click on **'Get Started'** under **'Business or Brand'** to start the process. The first thing you will need to do is enter the name of the Page. Think about this carefully as it is the name that people will see. There should be an option for you to change the URL, but nevertheless, choose wisely.

After you've chosen your name, you should choose the category that your business falls under. Fill out the details such as address, phone number, etc. and click on **'Continue'**.

As simple as that, you will be redirected to your new page. Follow Facebook's tips for customizing your page.

Profile Picture

The first step you need to take care of is to add a profile picture for your business. Think of this picture as your business' identity and make sure it is something that represents your company well, like a well-designed logo. Your profile picture is the first impression that your business gives on Facebook, so make sure it is recognizable.

It is recommended to upload a photo with 180 x 180 pixels, but do not worry if you don't have a square photo. Facebook will suggest cropping, but the important thing is that your entire logo (if uploading a logo) fits into the cropped picture.

Cover Photo

Your cover photo, the horizontal image that is found on the top of your page, in addition to your profile picture, is what gives personality to your page. Businesses usually use this photo to promote special offerings, discounts, etc.

To upload your cover photo just click the **'Add a cover photo'** button from your welcome menu. The best dimensions are 851 x 315 pixels, but again, you can adjust your photo directly on Facebook.

You can (and should!) update your cover photo on regular basis. To do so, just click the **'Change**

Cover' button found in the lower corner on the right of your current cover.

Description

To let people know what your business is all about, you will need a thoughtfully-written couple of sentences to introduce your brand. Facebook allows the maximum of 155 characters so choose your words carefully. Keep in mind that this description will also appear in the search results so make sure it is creatively descriptive.

Username

The username is the name that appears in your Facebook URL so help customers find you more easily. You have only 50 characters for your username; make sure to use them for something unique that is not already being used by other companies.

Setting Up the Roles

Now that the foundation of your page has been completed, it is time to set up the roles. The best thing about business pages is that they are kept completely separate from your personal Facebook account. That means that you are not the only person who can edit the page. Other people from your organization can also maintain the page without having to log in through your personal account. However, it is up to you to assign the roles.

Admin. The admin of the page manages pretty much everything. From sending messages, responding to comments, publishing and deleting posts, to advertising and even assigning the roles. This person should be someone you trust the most, so choose carefully.

Editor. Pretty much all permission as the admin, without the ability to assign roles.

Moderator. Moderators can respond and delete comments, but do not have the permission to post on the page. They are permitted to advertise on Facebook, though.

Advertiser. As the name suggests, the advertiser is only in charge of the advertising part.

Analyst. They are only allowed to track the posts and see which admin published what.

Live Contributor. The live contributor is someone that can go live (when live streaming), but does not have the permission to publish or respond to comments.

Call-to-Action

Call to action is a great benefit that Facebook provides. As of December 2014, Facebook allows Pages to include a CTA button, which is a very convenient way for customers to take action with your business. Click on **'Add a Button'** found above your cover and choose what the button should allow customers to do: get in touch, download an app, purchase a product, donate, book your services, etc. then add a link to direct them to your website, video, or another landing page.

Page Tabs

In order for you to organize the content that customers will see on your Page, it is recommended that you add custom tabs. That way your audience will have the chance to see your photos, check for open jobs, go to your website, visit your Pinterest, etc.

In your left navigation, there is a **'Manage Tabs'** button. Click on it to change your tabs.

Verify

Customers do not trust unverified pages, it's as simple as that. This is not absolutely required, but if you want to add more value to your page and include a degree of authority, it is recommended. Go to **'Settings'** → **'General'** → **'Page Verification'** to enter your phone number, country, etc. You will get a Facebook verification code to enter.

Getting Your Fans

Now that your Page is up and running, it is time for you to get your first likes. Getting a 'like' from a customer is them saying they are interested in what you are selling and that they want to keep in touch with your products/services and promotions. As the most successful business have millions of likes, your goal is to strive to get as many of those 'thumbs-ups' as possible.

Why Not Just Buy Likes?

It seems easier and more convenient, right? If you type "buying Facebook likes" on Google, you will be redirected to sites upon sites all selling packages of likes for a fixed price. You may be tricked into thinking that this will make your business look more successful and credible, but those likes are nothing but thin air. These so-called companies that sell these types of likes use fake or compromised accounts and click farms. You will not be getting actual likes from an audience that is interested in your product/service. It is really unlikely that any of them with engage with your content, so the only thing that buying them will get you is empty likes.

Promoting On Facebook

In order to get your likes, you need to make sure that you are actually promoting your Page on Facebook the right way. Here are some tips that will help you gain likes:

- Make sure your username and Page name is clear

- Go through the 'About' section and optimize. Include relevant keywords that will help people find you easier on Google and other search engines

- Share your Page with your friends and get them to like it

- Finally, be active and interact with the fans that you already have, as they will drive more traffic to your page

Promoting Through Your Website

If you are new to Facebook but have a website that already has a group of customers, do not forget to spread the word and promote your Facebook page there. You don't have to convince them to do so; adding a page plugin on your website with built-in Facebook iframe code will allow your audience to like or even share your page without actually leaving your website.

Promoting Directly to Your Customers

Another great way of promoting your Facebook page is directly to your customers. Have a store? Design a fabulous Facebook sticker with your logo on it to know people you are online. When sending emails to your customers, include your page's URL at the top corner of the message. You can also include the URL on your receipts. Want to get even more creative? Why not announce a promotion where you will offer discounted prices in return for a like on the spot.

Posting Like a Pro

We have already discussed the importance of quality posts. Your content is the core of social media marketing and as such, it should be posted regularly. Think of the posts as food for your Page. The more you feed it, the bigger it grows. But just as the food you eat, your posts should also be of high quality and carefully selected.

Besides the different types of content that we talked about earlier, there are also different ways to post on social media. Here are the different ways in which you can share your content with the world via Facebook:

Facebook Images

Studies have shown that Facebook image posts are 2.3 times more appealing and engaging to the audience, so that's a pretty good reason why you should share some quality images with your customers.

To post an image on Facebook is simple, simply click on **'Share a Photo or Video'** below the blank post space. Alternatively, you can start typing into the blank post and then click on the camera button on the left to upload your image.

The size of the images you are going to post is not that important (although 1200 x 3600 pixels is recommended). What's more important is the ratio. Make sure your ratio is 1.9:1 for best results.

Facebook Links

The best way to feed your Page is to share links to your products/services. Whether you are writing cooking blog posts or sell toys, your Facebook page needs to have links of your recent product/service in order for your customers to stay updated.

You can post a link the same way you post a written post. Just paste the link into the blank post space, and then write a short and engaging description. But wait before hitting 'Share' just yet. To make your Page look more professional, avoid keeping the URLs. Once the link has been uploaded, delete the URL so that your post looks clean.

Facebook Video

Did you know that it is predicted that Facebook will soon be all video? That's no surprise really since the number of daily video views is higher than 8 billion. There are over 100 million hours of Facebook videos that are watched every day. These are some powerful statistics that show us just how engaging videos are to people on Facebook.

To post a video, the process is the same as posting a photo. Click the **'Share a Photo or Video'** and then simply select the desired file from your computer. The recommended file format is MP4 and MOV. Then, add a line or two of text, describing or introducing the video to your audience.

Keep in mind that Facebook plays the first 5-10 seconds automatically, which means that even if a person is not thinking about watching a video, when scrolling down their news feed, they will see the beginning of your video. Try to make the beginning as appealing as possible in order to lure people to hit the play button and watch the whole thing.

Facebook Live

Unlike posting pre-produced videos, Facebook live is a feature that allows you to stream live videos via your smartphone. To give this a try, open the Facebook app on your phone and go to your Page. Click the **'Publish'** button and then choose the **'Live Video'** option. Once you allow Facebook to access your camera and microphone, select **'Continue'**.

Before you actually start streaming, you need to enter some privacy settings. You can choose whether to stream to friends, the whole public or just to yourself. Once you choose that, you should write a line or two compelling people to watch your video. The line will go alongside your streaming, so make sure it is unique and descriptive.

When ready to roll, hit **'Go Live'** and voila… You are on the air.

When you are done streaming, select **'Finish'.** This will end the streaming but will keep a recording on your Page for later watching.

Bu connecting with the audience this way, you show them that you care not only about making a profit, but also about their opinion and satisfaction. Engaging with your customers through Facebook Live can turn out to be a great marketing trick.

Facebook Instant Articles

Just like suggested in its name, Facebook Instant Articles means reading articles on the spot, without having to leave Facebook and be redirected to another site. This feature is great because it saves time and it is pretty convenient.

Not all businesses can take advantage of Instant Articles, but if you happen to be a publisher, this can throw a lot of good things your way.

Virtual Reality

Virtual reality for Facebook is something that you absolutely have to try if you have a mesmerizing story to tell. And if you need to promote a special place or an important experience of some kind, then you really cannot afford to pass out on this feature. Facebook Virtual Reality allows you to post 360-degrees videos for a full enjoyment. This works best on mobile and it is the most appreciated if recorded with a 360-degree camera, so think about investing in a Ricoh Theta or Allie camera as a part of your killer marketing strategy.

PIN YOUR POSTS

Pinning your posts means choosing the order in which they will appear on your page. Facebook offers an option to pin a post to the top of your page so that your most important announcements/promotions are the first thing that attracts the customer's eye when they visit your Page.

Try this out by clicking on the arrow found on the top right corner of a post you have previously shared. Then, simply click on **'Pin to Top of Page'.** Until you pin another post, this is the post that will be shown at the top of your Page.

Optimizing for SEO

If you are wondering whether your Facebook Page can affect your Google ranking, stop, because it does. And I am sure it has a way bigger impact than what you can imagine. Here is the role that a successful Facebook Page can play in Search Engine Optimization (SEO):

- It can drive traffic to your website

- It can attract a highly relevant audience interested in what you are selling

- It builds links through your Facebook shares

- It can improve your visibility with the help of optimized keywords

And if you are still not sure how this process works, here is an example:

1. You post your content on Facebook *(provide value)*

2. Your customers share your posts *(building links)*

3. The friends of your friends notice your content *(boosting visibility)*

4. The friends of your friends then click to see the content *(higher click-through rates)*

5. More people visit your website *(higher traffic)*

6. More people engage with your business *(low bounce rate)*

55

This simple example clearly shows you the importance of Facebook Marketing for your ranking on the search engines.

Keywords, Keywords, Keywords

Your Facebook content can be successfully optimized by using relevant keywords. You may have noticed how Google also lists social media results when searching for keywords. For instance, if you type *organic cotton clothing company,* you will get results for websites and social media networks of the top organic cotton clothing companies. That is because these companies have optimized their Pages and websites and included the relevant keywords *organic, cotton, clothing,* and *company,* which is how you will actually find them online.

Optimizing your content on Facebook will help people discover you and learn about your business easily. But how can you do that? There are three different ways in which you can add proper keywords and improve your business' visibility:

#1: Optimize Your URL

Make sure that your Page's URL contains the keywords that people will most likely use to search for your business online.

#2: Optimize Your 'About' Section

You may not know this, but what you write under 'About' on Facebook can also help people discover you online. Here is how you can ensure that your 'About' section is optimized:

- Conduct research to see what are the most relevant keywords for your business

- Choose 2 of the most relevant keywords

- Write your description creatively, mentioning these keywords a few time

- Make sure your Business Info is completed. Often times business' Pages are not listed at the top of Google Results because of lack of details. Make sure to enter your exact location, phone number, website, and other important info that will help customers find you.

Tip: Stay natural! Your description should contain the relevant keywords but at the same time sound warm and appealing. Do not go overboard with the keywords you find.

#3: Optimize the Post You Share

This is perhaps the trickiest part as the attempt to optimize your posts should be continuous and implemented on each post you think about sharing.

Just like your 'About' section, your post should also contain relevant keywords. For instance, if you are promoting a new product, conduct research to see what the most relevant keywords for that kind of products are, and include them in your post. If you are not an SEO guru, then you should seriously think about hiring an expert to have at your disposal.

The Right Marketing Strategy

And now, let's talk some real business. Now that you know what your posts should look like and how to optimize them for best results, it is time for the real challenge of Facebook marketing – finding the right strategy, or in other words, what and when to post.

Assuming that you already know who your audience is, let's move forward and talk some real strategies.

*If you don't know the persona of your audience, you can use a tool called **Audience Insights**. This amazing tool will help you obtain behavioral, as well as demographic data of your audience, in order to determine what kind of posts people are actually looking for.*

Social Media Content Calendar

If you are not using a social media management tool, then you absolutely need to have a content calendar for your Facebook posts. It doesn't have to

59

be anything fancy. Your content calendar can be a simple spreadsheet where you will write your posts in advance and appoint them for different times. Here are some tips for a great Social Media Content Calendar:

- Have tabs for each of your platforms (This calendar is not only for Facebook but your other Social Media Networks as well)

- Have a day-by-day post plan that is divided into time slots

- Leave some columns for specific details such as the name of the campaign, images you wish to post alongside, the count of characters, a short note to remember, etc.

- In order to keep track of large campaigns, leave room for a monthly view of your posts

Scheduling Your Posts

Although having a social media calendar can be a real life-saver when it comes to social media marketing, you will never be able to take a break if you do not actually schedule your posts on Facebook. If you plan on successfully marketing on this platform, you will need to be super-active and post regularly. That can be tricky if you are crunched for time and not always available. Thankfully, Facebook offers a great option that allows you to schedule your posts ahead of time.

The process is pretty simple. Instead of hitting **'Publish'** and sharing your post after it has been written, click on the arrow found next to **'Publish'** and select **'Schedule'** instead. Enter the time and date, and you are all set.

If you have a change of hearts, do not worry, you can always reschedule or cancel. Just click on **'Publishing Tools'** that's found at the top of your Page and choose to *Reschedule, Cancel Schedule, Backdate,* or *Delete.*

When to Post and How Often?

Scheduling your posts is great, but if you do not actually know when the right time for posting is, it may not turn out to be that beneficial. So, when is

61

the right time to post on Facebook? And how often should you share your posts?

If you came here looking for a clear-cut answer that will apply to your business, let me break it to you – there isn't one. When and how often to post on Facebook depends on many factors: whether you audience is in the same time zone, your location, your main goal, what your business is about, etc. However, there are some tricks to have up your sleeve.

Stick to the Rules of Thumb

WHEN TO POST:

- The rule of a thumb is that your posts will be seen by more people if you shoot for between 1 p.m. and 5 p.m. on weekdays, and between noon and 1 p.m. on the weekends.

- The best days for posting on Facebook are Saturday and Sunday, followed by Friday and Thursday, so save your most important posts for these days.

- People seem to be happier on Fridays, so save your cheerful and upbeat posts for this day.

- Statistics say that posting on Facebook at 3 p.m. will get you the most likes, while the 1 p.m. posts will bring you more shares, so have this in mind when posting.

HOW OFTEN TO POST:

When it comes to how often your posts should be, the rule of a thumb is between 1 and 2 posts per day. You may think that posting frequently will bring more engagement, but it is quite the opposite, actually. Studies have shown that frequent posts bring a decrease in audience.

Another rule of a thumb is that posting more than 1-2 times a day can be beneficial only for the successful companies that have more than 10,000 followers. Posting more than 2 times a day for companies that have less than 10,000 likes can bring 60% fewer clicks, statistics show.

You need to remember that quality trumps always trumps quantity, so do not obsess yourself with how frequent your posts should be. Instead, make sure that your content is well-crafted, created for the right audience, and consistent.

Facebook Bots

A bot is an AI program that people communicate with in order to ask for some info or automatically complete a certain task. Facebook bots have completely taken over the Messenger and are especially important for businesses.

The same way people use Messenger to chat with friends, they can also use this platform to communicate with bots in order to ask for updates, change a shipping address, ask for working hours, order items, etc. By getting rid of never-ending scrolling down the company's page in order to find what they are looking for, communicating with bots makes the shopping experience much more convenient for customers. In fact, half of the people are interested in shopping from an artificial bot, so make sure you add a chatbot to your Facebook Page.

There are a lot of platforms that can help you create a chatbot. Chatfuel.com is one of the most popular ones.

Generating Leads

Leads are potential customers. They are those people that have already shown interest in your product or service but are not paying customers just yet. For instance, if someone has subscribed for a free trial, have downloaded a free chapter of your eBook, or has signed up for a demo product, that person is a *lead.*

In order for you to actually turn your leads into customers, you need to have a good strategy about how to generate leads and post content that they will find attractive:

- Posting landing pages for special offers

- Scheduling Facebook events for an upcoming webinar

- Creating and posting videos that will advertise special lead generation offers

- Posting Facebook Lives in order to remind your audience for upcoming events

- Share blog posts that have already proven to generate leads

Of course, you need to be careful not to overdo it. Not all of your content should be lead generation. Mix things up and come up with the right balance that works best for your business.

Facebook Lead Ads can be used in order to gather Facebook lead info. This is a great feature that will grant access of your special offers to your audience, without the need to leave the Facebook app.

Tracking Your Results

Now that you know a few tricks that can get you more clicks, likes, and shares, it is time to learn how you can check to see if your marketing efforts really pay out. Your marketing strategy will not a proper plan for tracking the results will involve a lot of guesses and maybes, which can result in underachievement.

For that purpose, Facebook has created a great tool call *Facebook Insights* that can help you analyze, track, and measure your success.

To enter this tool, select the **'Insights'** tab that is found at the top of your page. Once you do that you will be brought to the **'Overview'** of your Page, which is your Page's activity for the last week. You can take a look at this, but if you want to check out some more specific details, you will need to go through the tabs on the left.

Likes. The Like section will show you how many likes you've received so far for each day. You will see a graph that will show your performance. There you will find the **Net Likes** graph, which is what you should be interested in most, and that is the number of likes minus the number of unlikes.

Reach. If you want to see how people engage with your content, check out the **Reach** tab. There you will find a graph of post engagement that is divided into organic traffic (traffic that occurs naturally) and paid traffic (the traffic that you pay for and target directly to specific consumers through advertising).

Page Views. This will not only show you the number of times your page has been visited, but also how those people got to your Page. Additionally, here, you can also learn about what people usually do after landing on your Page.

Posts. This is probably the most useful option that this tool offer, as it helps you learn about when your followers are online, which can be super helpful during your process of scheduling posts.

Posts show your fans reactions, comments, shares, post hides, reports or spams, engagement rate, etc.

If you want a quick check of the success of your posts without having to go through Page Insights, simply click on **'People Reached'** that is find right above the **'Like'** button, and you can go through post details immediately.

Advertising on Facebook

To advertise your products or services on Facebook, you have to complete a process of three different elements:

1. Campaign

2. Ad Sets

3. Ads

This chapter will help you learn all about Facebook advertising and how to maximize the results with the minimum budget and effort.

Facebook Ad Campaign

Before you begin the process of creating an ad, Facebook will ask you to select your editor of choice, which will be Ad Manager or Power Editor. They both have their ups and downs, depending on what you are looking for. The Ad Manager is used the most as it is more versatile, but if you are a large company and looking for increased precision and control over multiple campaigns, then Power Editor may be a better fit.

For this purpose, let's imagine that you are satisfied with Ad Manager. In the right upper corner of your Page there is a drop-down menu. Click on it, and then select **'Create Ads'**.

There, you will be prompted to choose an objective for your campaign. You will find 11 objectives in total, divided into 3 categories. Choose the one that suits you the most. The initial process of starting a campaign has been completed.

The Ad-Sets

Once the initial process is over, you should then go through the steps of defining your audience, setting the budget, and scheduling and optimizing the ad set.

Audience

If you have used this tool before, chances are your audience is already remembered by Facebook. If not, enter specified info like gender, age, location, and language of your target audience. After that, you can add more filters by, for instance, targeting only the audience that has liked a specific page, or something like that.

Make sure that it is the **'Automatic Placements'** selected under **'Placements'.**

Budget

There are two budget typed to choose from:

Daily Budget – If your goal is to advertise continuously, then choose this option. Enter the amount that you are comfortable with spending on daily basis for this specific ad.

Lifetime Budget – Choose this option if you have a specified amount of time that you wish to run the ad for. Here, your budget will be spread evenly for that time period.

Schedule

Now it's time to schedule your ad set. You can either choose to start the advertising process immediately or schedule a start and end date for your ad.

Optimization

Click the **'Show Advanced Options'** button and choose your preferred optimization. Here, you choose the option that you want your advertisement to be optimized for so that Facebook can show the add to people that will pay attention the most.

If you are all set, click **'Continue'**

Creating the Ad

Now it is time to select the format, text, media, and links, and create your Facebook ad:

1. First of all, choose your desired format options. Facebook will show you suggestions (carousel, single image, slideshow, single video, etc.) so select the one that looks the most appealing to you.

2. Now that you have selected the look of your ad, upload the assets and write a captivating ad headline. Facebook will give recommendations for the design based on the selected format.

3. Tweak, polish, preview, and finally, finish the creation.

Tips for Successful Advertising

Here are some tips that can boost your advertisement process and, in turn, boost both the organic ad paid traffic:

Focus on Videos

Video ads bring far more clicks than the image-based ones. How-to videos, customer-testimonial videos, and tasteful product demonstration videos can help you generate a lot of business.

Go for Lookalike Audience

A lookalike audience is a group of people that is very similar to another group. This is a great advertisement trick, as you can actually create a list of customers (or even leads) and upload that to Facebook to create your lookalike audience. To upload this, go to your Ad Manager, open **'Audiences'** and choose the **'Lookalike Audience'** option.

When Retargeting, Be Specific

When retargeting your audience, do not just retarget them as a group, but try to get as specific as possible. Depending on what you are advertising, try to choose, for instance, only those people that have visited a specific part of your website, or purchased a specific type of product.

Install the Facebook Pixel

Facebook Pixel, the key tool for Facebook advertising, is a simple code that you place on your website that collects the data and enables you not only to keep a track of your conversions, but also to build audiences, optimize your ads, and even remarket.

To create your Facebook Pixel, go to your **'Facebook Events Manager'** and choose **'Pixels'**. Then, click on **'Create a Pixel'**, enter the name of your Pixel, and click on **'Create'.**

To add the Pixel to your website, you will need to install some codes on your website, but that mainly depends on the platform you use.

If you are using an e-commerce platform, this can be done easily as Facebook will offer you a Help article that will explain the whole process.

75

If you are working with a developer, you can choose the option to **Email Instructions to Developer.**

You can also choose to **Manually Install the Code Yourself**, in which case you will need to copy and paste the code into your website's header code.

Try the Callout Method

It may sound clichéd, but calling out for people's attention seems to be a trick that's as old as time. But who cares as long as it works? Try to start the ad with a couple of questions that will call out your audience.

For instance, if you are promoting your weight-loss book, you may want to start like this: "Tired of eating bland greens for the sake of your flat belly? Want to have both- a satisfied tummy and a lean figure? I have the perfect solution for you…" and then add a couple of words that describe your book.

Another perk of this method is that it can serve as an additional tool for targeting audience. Here, for example, the target audience are those people whose diets are inefficient, who are always hungry and miserable and are looking for a better way to lose weight. Which is exactly what you are offering.

Stick to the 20%-or-Less Text Rule

It was a Facebook's rule to automatically disapprove those image ads that had more than 20 percent of text. They might not be so strict anymore and sometimes even allow such ads, however, it is a fact that people respond better to the visual. Try to keep the text to a minimum by choosing the right words carefully, and make the image the star of your advertisement.

The Boost Post

Although not exactly an advertising strategy, the **'Boost Post'** option that Facebook offers is another great way in which you can, well, boost your post. When to use this? Unless you are a super successful company with millions of fans, chances are you need to press the 'Boost Post' from time to time.

When your post does not drag enough traffic to your page, it is time to use additional tools to boost your organic reach. The 'boost post' button will not only help you increase your organic traffic, but it will also give you the opportunity to reach a wider audience.

Of course, boosting your post and promoting it on Facebook will cost you some money. But if you think that it'll break the bank, you cannot be more wrong. Just like with Facebook ads, you get to set your own budget, so in the end, you pay the amount that you are actually comfortable with. The minimum amount is $1 per week, but keep in mind that the more money you spend, the wider your targeted audience will be.

Step 1: Choose Your Post

Whether it is the one you are crafting at the moment or an earlier post, choose the one you want to present to your audience and hit the **'Boost Post'** button that is found in the lower right corner of your post of your choice.

Step 2: Target Your Audience

After choosing the post you wish to boost, Facebook will give you the option to choose options for targeting the right audience for you. You can easily create a custom audience by selecting the **'Create New Audience'** option and defining it as you would like by setting the age range, location, specific interests, and other important factors.

Step 3: Set Your Budget

After defining your audience, you should have a pretty realistic idea of how much you need to spend for your boosted post. Again, you can spend the minimum of $1, but know that higher budget equals to higher reach.

Step 4: Set the Duration

You will then need to select the number of days you want your post to be boosted. The default is set for 1, 7, and 14 days, but you can also enter a specified date.

Step 5: Preview the Boosted Post

Now is the time for you to take a look at your ad and make sure that everything looks good (links work, it is error-free, etc.) as this is your last chance to correct any mistakes before your post actually goes live.

Step 6: Choose Your Payment Option

Choose the method in which you are planning to pay for your boost posts. Fill out the details and click **'Continue'.**

Step 7: Boost

Finally, you are ready to boost. To check the status of the post you have boosted, you can check out the **'Delivery'** column under **'Ads Manager'**

YouTube

I am certain that everyone who has ever used the Internet is aware of how huge YouTube is. In fact, I am also pretty sure that, at some point, we have all wasted an entire lazy day watching funny YouTube videos. But what not everyone knows is that, besides its ability to entertain, this platform has also become a crucial tool for successful marketers from all over the world.

With over 1.8 billion monthly users (who are actually logged-in), over 1 billion of hours of watched videos per day, and over 400 hours' worth of video being uploaded every minute, YouTube is the 2nd largest search engine.

Whatever category they might fall under, chances are, a huge chunk of your target audience is already on YouTube. Marketing your content on YouTube is a smart move that will help your brand grow by providing more value to your customers.

Creating Your Business Profile

Before we jump right to setting up your business YouTube Account and creating your profile, we first need to make sure that you have an active Google account. As you may know, YouTube is owned by Google, and by owning a Gmail account you can access YouTube logged-in.

But wait before opening YouTube and beginning the profile creation process. Tying up your YouTube profile to your already existing mail may not be such a good idea, especially if we are talking about your business Gmail account. Sharing your access to your YouTube profile with everyone in your company who has access to your business email is not that recommended. For that purpose, it is smart to open a different Gmail account:

1. Go to www.google.com and select the **'Sign In'** button found in the upper right corner.

2. Go to **'Create'** → **'Create Account'**.

3. Fill out the details by entering your name, the name of the email, password, birthday, etc. and click on **'Next Step'.**

4. Verify your account by entering your phone number where a code number will be sent. Type in the code and click **'Continue'.** Your new Gmail account is now up and running.

Now that you have a Gmail account, it is time to set up the actual YouTube account for your brand and create its profile.

To get started, simply, visit www.youtube.com. If you are logged in with your Gmail, then you are probably already logged in with YouTube. If not, click on the **'Sign In'** button in the upper right corner and enter your Gmail and its password. Once you are in, click on the button of your Gmail account in the upper right corner, and select **'My Channel'.** You will have the option to create your channel right away, but for your purpose, choose **'Use a Business or Other Name'** from the bottom of the page. Now, enter the name of your brand and then click **'Create'**. Keep in mind that this can be updated later from your settings menu.

Channel Icon and Channel Art

Now that your channel is created, it is time to customize it. Simply select the **'Edit Layout'** and let's get started. The first thing you need to do is to create a channel icon and art. Channel icon and channel art for YouTube are what the profile picture and cover image are for Facebook – they are the first thing that your visitors see and therefore leave the first impression.

Click on the default red picture to add your channel icon. Choose a file from your computer, but keep in mind that this picture will be used on your Grail and Google+ accounts as well. 800 x 800 pixels are recommended here.

Next, click on the **'Add channel art'** button found in the center of your channel and upload your preferred image. Here, 2560 x 1440 pixels are recommended.

Describing Your Brand

After uploading your pictures, it is time to add some details about your business and customize the **'About'** tab. Write a gripping and compelling description that will explain your business briefly and also let people know about the type of videos that will be uploaded on your channel. Make sure to include links to your website and other social media platforms, as well as to include your business email address.

A great option that YouTube provides is the fact that you can customize your channel differently for unsubscribed and subscribed users. The best way to use this option is to add a *channel trailer* that will lure visitors to hit the 'subscribed' button.

The channel trailer is a video description of your channel and it should be short (not longer than 90 seconds; 45 seconds is the best) and appealing. Its main purpose should be to welcome visitors and encourage them to subscribe.

Once you make your channel trailer, it is time to upload it:

1. Make sure that the channel customization is on. You can check this after clicking the settings icon next to 'Subscribe'. Click **'Customize the layout of your channel'** and then hit **'Save'**.

2. Click on the arrow button found in the upper right corner to upload your trailer. Choose the right file from your computer and click on **'For New Users'** once it uploads.

3. Select **'Channel Trailer'**, choose the file you've uploaded, and hit **'Save'.**

Once you get your first 100 subscribers, your channel is more than 30 days old, and you have a channel icon and art uploaded, your YouTube profile will become eligible for a unique and

86

custom URL, which will give it a more professional look.

Appointing the Roles

Before you actually start uploading videos and begin your YouTube marketing strategy, you need to specify how many members of your team will have access to your brand's YouTube channel and what their roles will be.

Once you give them access to the Google account, there are three different role options:

Owner – They will have full power meaning they can add/remove managers, respond/delete comments or reviews, edit information, etc.

Manager – Managers can have all of the editing access as the owner, without the ability to add or remove other managers.

Communications Manager – As the name suggests, the communications manager is mainly in charge of communicating with the audience. They can respond to comments and reviews and do some other editing options, however, they cannot upload new content, view the analytics, or use the video manager.

Go to **'Overview'** → **'Add or remove managers'** and add individuals to manage your YouTube account.

Optimizing for SEO

So, you've successfully created your YouTube business channel. Congratulations! But there is so much more to successful marketing than just creating and uploading engaging videos. For people to watch your videos, they will have to find them first. And how can they do so if you haven't optimized the metadata of your videos?

The metadata of your videos is what gives people information about the video such as its title, category, thumbnail, tags, description, subtitles, etc. and providing the right kind of metadata will help your audience discover your video easily, whether on YouTube or Google search.

Title

When scrolling through the results on YouTube, the first thing that people notice about a video are its title and thumbnail. The title is what hooks the viewer's attention and therefore should be well-thought-out. Conduct a research to understand what it is that people are looking for. Then, include the relevant keywords and important information in the title, but be careful not to go overboard. If your title has more than 60 characters, it will be shown cut-off in the video result pages on YouTube, and people may not even read the whole thing. Keep it simple, clear, and extremely compelling.

Description

Just like your title, the description of the video should also contain relevant keywords that will help potential viewers discover your video easily. But as important as the description is, you need to keep in mind that most people do not actually bother to read it. Unless they are interested, that is. Your job is to make them interested. YouTube usually shows only the first 2-3 lines of the description. If viewers want to read the rest of it, they have to click the 'show more' button for the remaining content. Make sure to polish and re-polish the beginning of the description as much as it takes for it to be compelling so that your viewers would want to read the entire content.

If your description contains CTAs or some important links that you want to share with your audience, make sure to include them in the beginning of the description where people will be able to see them even without clicking 'show more'.

Another thing when it comes to writing the description, it is important to always include a transcript of your video. Why? Because your video itself is filled with keywords. By writing a short transcript with these keywords you will significantly improve your SEO and eventually, your brand's ranking.

Tags

Tags are great because they can associate your brand's videos with other, similar videos on YouTube, which only widens their reach and improves your visibility. For that purpose, make sure that your important keywords are tagged. Highlighting the most relevant keywords first is a crucial part of your brand's SEO optimization so make sure to choose your words wisely.

Category

Once your video is uploaded, you will need to choose the category under which it will be shown on YouTube. You can choose the video's category under **'Advanced settings'**. You can choose from Film & Animation, Travel & Events, Entertainment, Music, Pets & Animals, Educations, Nonprofits & Activism, People & Blogs, Sports,

Autos & Vehicles, How-to & Style, Science & Technology, News & Politics, and Comedy.

Choosing your category carefully is very important as the categories are what group your videos with the relevant ones on YouTube. For instance, if you are selling dog shampoo and list your video under People & Blogs instead of Pets & Animals, you may not reach your target audience.

Thumbnail

As mentioned earlier, the thumbnail of your video is extremely important as it is, along with the title, the first thing that people see on YouTube after discovering your video. The thumbnails have a significant impact on the number of views and should be selected carefully. Although YouTube will recommend an option of a few auto-generated thumbnails after uploading, it is highly recommended to skip this option and include a custom thumbnail instead. Choose a shot that will encourage people to click and that represents your video in a good light. YouTube says that 90% of the most successful videos on YouTube actually have custom thumbnails, so you cannot be wrong with this one.

SRT Files

Closed captions and subtitles are extremely helpful for viewers, but that is not the only reason why your video should include them. SRT files are also a great way for you to highlight your keywords. Whether you choose to add a timed subtitles file or a transcript of your text, SRT files are a valuable SEO optimization tool that you should definitely take advantage of.

To add SRT files go to **'Video Manager'** → **'Videos'**. There, choose the video to which you want to add the SRT files and select the drop-down arrow on the right. Select **'Subtitles/CC'** and choose accordingly.

End Screens and Cards

Adding end screens and cards is a valuable option offered by YouTube that can help you encourage your viewers to visit your website, check out your other videos, and even to answer poll questions.

Cards are the small notifications that usually appear in the upper right corner of your video. Your card can contain a poll, a link, another video, or can be used to promote another channel on YouTube. You can add up to 5 cards at the same time, but be careful as too many inquiries have the tendency to put off viewers. If you absolutely must add a few cards, make sure to space them out well so that your viewers can take several actions without feeling overwhelmed.

To add a card go to **'Video Manager'** ➔ **'Cards'** ➔ **'Add Card'** and choose whether you want to create a Link, Video or Playlist, Channel, or a Poll card. After creation, simply drag the card to where you want it to appear on the video.

End Screens are those last seconds of the video that encourage the viewers to take further action such as subscribe to channel, visit a Facebook page, click the like button, check out another video, etc. You

94

can add 5-20 extra seconds to your videos and ask your viewers to engage with your brand.

To add an end screen go to **'Video Manager'**, click on the drop-down arrow then choose **'End Screens and Annotations'**. There, you can choose which elements you want your end screen to include, just keep in mind that it is required to promote another YouTube video or a playlist, so even if you only wanted to encourage viewers to visit your website, you'd have to also encourage people to watch some other video of your brand there.

Playlists

You may think that creating playlists is not worth your time, but this feature is a real gem for the YouTube marketers. Why? Because it increases your visibility. By creating your playlists, you can combine videos not only from your channels but other YouTube channels as well. And the best part is that these playlists are listed and shown separately in the search results. For instance, if you make a collection of your videos and include some popular ones with similar content, you will help other people who may not have heard about your brand before, discover you.

To create a playlist, click on the '+' button under your video, select **'Create new playlist',** choose the name for your playlist, and click on **'Create'**. To add more videos, simply use the same button but instead of clicking on 'Create new playlist' choose the already existing one to feature your videos there.

Making the Videos

Now that your YouTube channel is all set up and know what you have to do in order to optimize it for SEO, the next step is to learn how to make killer videos that people will actually watch. After all, those videos that are of high quality are the most important part of YouTube marketing. Your high-class strategy will not have much value if your videos are not created carefully, addressing the right audience.

So let's start enriching your channel with amazing content, shall we?

Type of YouTube Videos

Before you say "Action" and actually start filming, first you need to determine what the type of your video will be. There are eight types of videos that YouTube marketers usually create:

1. Customer Testimonials

Customer testimonials are something that every successful brand should film at some point and upload to their YouTube channel. They are short interview-like videos where content customers are filmed to express their satisfaction with the product/service, share their positive experience with others, as well as recommend the brand to anyone who is considering their products or services.

2. Explainer Videos

Explainer videos are also called *tutorial videos* or *how-to videos* and their main purpose, as the name suggests, is to explain to customers how to use a particular product or service. They are also a very detailed and thoughtful way to explain some more complex customer support questions.

3. On-Demand Demonstration Videos

Demonstration videos are usually short videos filmed with the purpose to briefly demonstrate the use of a particular product or service, as well as to reveal its benefits to potential customers.

4. Case Studies and Project Reviews

Whether it is the case studies of a successful campaign or the 5-star reviews of a certain product, the purpose of these videos is to recap the positive results and share them with the world in order to turn potential customers into buyers.

5. Thought Leader Interviews

These videos are quality interview with experts of your niche with the sole purpose of increasing the credibility of your brand.

6. Video Blogs

Video blogs or usually called *vlogs* are frequently posted videos (on a daily or weekly basis), documenting some events. Video blogs are popular among the YouTube marketers because they are a great way to get people to visit your website. By summarizing a certain blog post and uploading the video to your YouTube channel, you also give your customers multiple options in which they can absorb your content.

7. YouTube Live

YouTube Live is a feature that allows you to broadcast live to your subscribers. This amazing feature is of extreme value for your marketing strategy because it allows you to connect with your audience live, and lets them engage in real-time discussions.

8. Event Videos

Event videos are those videos that show some experience of a conference, auction, or some other event, and are a great way to share the positive reaction of the present crowd to your online viewers.

The Script of Your Videos

Now that you've chosen the type of your video, it is time to carefully craft its script. Before you start filming, there are a couple of steps that you need to take care of in order to ensure that the video will provide value.

The Goal

Before you turn your idea into reality, you need to determine first what that idea should accomplish. What is the goal of your video? What are you trying to achieve by uploading it to your channel? Do you want to increase the number of subscribers? Enhance your brand's awareness? Drive more traffic to your website?

Of course, you want all those things, but the key to making a successful video that will be watched, is a singular goal. Make each video with a single goal in mind. This will help you stay focused and prevent tackling different things at one time, which is the best marketing practice there is.

Create the Story

Now for the creative part. After determining your goal, it is time to wake up your imagination and craft a good story for your video. This should serve as a blueprint and an outline that will be followed during the shooting process. A good video storyboard should include:

- A frame for each scene

- A short description for each of the scenes

- The lines for each of the scenes

- Camera directions and details for the shooting (for instance, wide shots, tight shots, etc.)

The Extra Elements

If you are planning to include some additional multimedia elements in your videos such as slides or graphics, then you should plan for them in advance. Make sure that the extra content will be placed without any errors and add them to your storyboard.

The Length of the Video

How long will your video be? This is an important factor in the video making process so make sure to determine this as early as possible. Videos under 2 minutes have the highest degree of audience engagement on YouTube, so keep that in mind when deciding on how long it will take for you to deliver the key message.

The Filming Location

Depending on the type and concept of your video, you may need one, two or several filming locations. Finding the perfect shooting spot can be tricky, so you might want to involve your friends and family to help you out with this one. Whatever you choose, remember that for some locations you may need a shooting permit, so take care of this one beforehand to avoid being sued.

Before shooting, visit each of the locations to determine how to adjust the scenery, take care of the lighting, pay attention to the ambient sounds, etc.

Shooting a High-Quality Video

Unless you are a very successful company and can afford to pay a fancy filming crew to take care of the video making process for you, chances are, you will need some pro tips that will help you make high-quality videos that will be watchable. Whether you are using your smartphone or a semi-professional camera for recording, the tips below will help you populate your channel with professional content:

A Tripod Is a Must. The first impression is often the most important one, especially when trying to represent your brand and promote products/services. If your video starts with a shaky camera, no one will watch it, period. When clicking on the video, people are looking to hear the story behind it, not to be distracted by the unprofessional shooting. If your shot is static, buy a decent tripod that will hold your camera steady for a professional look.

Go for Different Angles. A scene that is shot from only one angle is visually boring. To spice things up, shot each scene from a few different angles so you can edit afterward and create one appealing, expensive-like video.

More is More. Make a habit to always shoot more than you need. That will only give you more material to choose from during the editing process and will cost nothing but a bit more time. After all, it is always easy to cut out what you don't need. Going back and re-filming is not only a hassle but sometimes impossible.

Choose the Manual Mode. I've read somewhere that real photographers use only manual mode because they get to tell the camera what they want and there are no inconvenient surprises like with automation. If your camera has that option, go for a full manual mode to get the most out of filming. That way you can easily adjust the focus and shoot a visually-appealing video.

Invest in Your Microphone. If your video includes speaking, then investing in a high-quality microphone is not an option – it is a must. You don't want to sound like you are talking to your viewers from the end of a tunnel. Even if you are using your smartphone for the video making process, you can purchase a mic that can be plugged into your device and further enhance the sound of your video.

Editing Your Video

After filming, it is time to edit the video material and create a compelling video of high quality to upload to your YouTube channel.

Editing Tools. Chances are, your OS already has some editing software that offers basic tools for editing such as correction of color, cutting clips, or adding titles. However, if you want a video with a

105

more professional look, then spending some money on a more advanced software such as Adobe Premier CC or Final Cut Pro X, is highly recommended. If you want to keep things pretty low-budget, YouTube also offers online editing software for that purpose.

Thumbnails. As discussed earlier, video thumbnails are extremely important. The video thumbnail is what potential viewers will see in their video search results, on your YouTube channel, as well as their suggested column on their right when watching similar videos. The most successful YouTube marketers have their own custom-made thumbnails uploaded, so get creative and make one yourself.

Watermarks. Want to further encourage your viewers to hit the 'subscribe' button? Then adding a watermark is a perfect choice. Watermarks are custom-made 'subscribe' buttons that are placed on your videos with the purpose of attracting the viewer's eye and encouraging them to press conveniently and subscribe to your channel while watching your video.

If you want to add a watermark, go to **'Creator Studio'** → **'Channel'** → **'Branding'**. Press **'Add a Watermark'** and follow the uploading instructions.

Sound Effects. High-quality sound effects are probably the most important factor that makes the difference between a professional-shot video and an amateur one on a low budget. But you don't have to have a giant budget in order to include movie-like music. Now there are many ways to add a quality sound to your videos without draining your budget.

YouTube itself offers a variety of sound effects of high quality to choose for your videos. But if you are not so crazy about that option, then finding royalty-free music online is perhaps your best solution. There are royalty-free sounds that you can actually download for free, but if you want to add a more professional tone to your videos, then think about investing some money and download the right music for your video for a flat price. Royalty-free means that, once you pay for the download, you are free to use the music file any way you see fit, without having to make additional payments, even if your video skyrockets on YouTube.

Marketing the Videos

Now that your video is filmed, beautifully edited, and successfully uploaded to your YouTube channel, the next step is to find the best marketing strategy and get people to actually click on your video and watch it.

In case you haven't noticed, we've already covered a large chunk of YouTube marketing strategies that will help people discover and watch your videos such as: using relevant keywords, using tags, have a rich and compelling description, have the perfect thumbnail image, include descriptive transcripts, use cards and end screens, and combine your videos with popular ones in playlists. All of these, let's call them tricks, will help you boost the organic traffic, get more views, and improve your ranking. But if you have just embarked the YouTube marketing train, it might be pretty hard to stand out and achieve your goals. The initial (and the most important!) strategy for YouTube marketing is knowing how to *spread the word.*

Spreading the word and letting your audience know that you actually have a YouTube channel where they can check out your videos, is the first thing you need to take care of.

Social Media

Have a Facebook or Instagram account? Sharing your videos on other social media platforms is the best way to let your followers there know about your channel and videos and get them to engage. Fortunately, sharing YouTube videos couldn't be easier. To share a video, simply click the **'Share'** button found underneath the video and select the platform where you want to market the video. Another way is to copy the video URL from the address bar while the video is playing, and then paste the link on your social media page.

But keep in mind that sharing the video alone is not a good marketing strategy. You are not sharing a silly cat video with your friends; you need people to watch and engage. When thinking about sharing a video, also think about why you created the video in the first place. Was it a tutorial to simplify the use and answer some customer questions? If so, the best way is to share your video as a response to that questions. Was it a part of some trend or a campaign? If that was the reason, then do not forget the important #hashtags to ensure that your video is a part of a conversation. And if you simply want to spread awareness around your company, then including the link to the video in your 'About' section as well can be quite beneficial.

Website

Your website or blog is the perfect place for you to market your YouTube channel and videos. If you have a website that is up and running, do not forget to include 'Follow' icons to your social media platforms. This includes YouTube as well. This will help your blog's visitors to easily find your channel and click the 'Subscribe' button to stay updated with your video posts as well.

A great strategy is to also create a video that will be posted as an addition to a certain review, case study, or simply your blog post. This works well both ways because it can not only help you market your videos and gain more views on YouTube, but it can also drive organic traffic to your website and other platforms as well.

To post one of your YouTube videos to your website, find the embed code underneath the video, copy it, and paste it where you want it to be featured.

Email

The worst mistake that marketers can make is getting preoccupied with attracting a new audience and forgetting about the customers that they already have. Once your YouTube channel is packed with some videos, it is time to share the news with your existing users/customers. And what better way to do so than with an email list? Send an email newsletter with helpful information and video and encourage your customers to engage with your brand. You don't like the idea of sending your customers links to your videos? How about inviting them to check out a certain website post where your YouTube video has already been embedded?

Collaboration

Sometimes the solution is in someone else's hands. If your brand is in collaboration with another company that also has a YouTube channel, ask them to collaborate together. This will not only be fun and exciting for both companies, but it is the perfect way to join forces and expand your audience. By creating a video or even a playlist together, you may end up getting a lot of their subscribers and vice versa. The important thing to have in mind though, is that your goals are similar and that the collaboration with the other brand aligns with your strategy.

Q&A Websites

Have you ever visited a Q&A site? They are the perfect place to get a solution to your questions from experts and people that have experience in the field of your interest. www.quora.com is the most popular site right now. Take advantage of it. Monitor the kind of questions that people ask and provide solutions with your video content. Who knows? This might turn out to be your best marketing strategy out there.

Engage, Engage, Engage!

Finally, the solution can be pretty simple. Engage with your existing audience and get them to spread their satisfaction and positive experience. Answer their questions, respond to their comments in a timely manner, ask for their honest feedback, and do not forget to thank them for their support. This is the simplest but most easily forgotten task. Make sure to be there for the users so they can be there for you.

Getting a Handle on YouTube Analytics

Investing your time and effort into creating and uploading professional and helpful videos to your YouTube channel cannot possibly be successful if you are not measuring what you've achieved. Keeping a track of your success can help you pinpoint what you are doing wrong, what works best, and what needs to be improved in order to enhance the success and improve your YouTube ranking.

Every YouTube channel has its **YouTube Analytics** that contains reports of the channel's performance for a certain time period. Understanding exactly what those numbers and graphs mean can help you get a clear picture of whether people find your videos attractive or not. Here is a quick tutorial on how to use Analytics to measure success:

Your Goal

If you don't have a clear goal in mind, you cannot possibly expect to measure your success, because you don't have a standard for your measurements. Knowing exactly why you post your video (remember, one goal per video?) will help you imagine where you see your video to be and where it is actually standing. That way you can understand what areas need improvement and whether you should think about investing in paid ads to drive more traffic to your channel.

Now that you have reminded yourself of what how you expect your videos to perform, it is time to check out whether they have delivered or not. The first thing you need to do is open your YouTube Analytics. Just go to www.youtube.com/analytics (be sure you are logged in). Once you enter you should see a performance overview of your videos for the last 28 days. You can adjust the timeframe and filter the results by the key metrics from there.

Watch Time

Watch time is a report that shows you the total number of minutes that your audience spent watching your content, whether in total or by video. This is an extremely important factor because it is what directly impacts the YouTube ranking. If your video has a high watch time, you should expect it to be ranked high in the video search results.

Average View Duration

The average view duration (retention rate) represents the average percentage that your audience watches per view. To put it simply, it is not the same if a person watches the first 10 seconds or finish watching the entire video. The higher this percentage is, the higher are the chances that your audience will watch the video until the end. Cards and end screens can help you improve this numbers, so if you haven't already included them, go back here and take care of that.

116

Traffic Sources

This report will show you exactly how your viewers are discovering your video content online. Whether it was the YouTube search, YouTube ads, suggested video, or from an external platform (such as your website or Facebook page), this report will show you how most people landed there. This is a very valuable factor as it clearly shows you what marketing strategy works best and where you need to spend some more time and effort.

Demographics

The demographics report will show you a clear picture of what age group watches your videos the most. But that's not all. You can then break down these groups into geography or gender to further understand your audience and see if your YouTube viewers match your already established buyer persona, or if you need to adjust your goals or videos to hit your target audience better.

Engagement Reports

These reports will show you what it is that your audience engages with the most. Here, you can pinpoint the most viewed, shared, promoted, or commented videos. Plus, this report will also show you how your cards and end screens are performing so you can further optimize your videos.

Advertising on YouTube

So you've done everything that you could and yet, the YouTube Analytics' reports aren't as satisfying as you hoped for. Well, I hate to break it to you, but promoting on social media and embedding on your website and crossing your fingers that someone will watch your videos won't cut it. You need to take some serious action and foot the bill for a high YouTube ranking. That means advertising on YouTube.

Types of YouTube Ads

There are three different types of YouTube ads to invest in. Read on to choose the one that fits your needs and budget the most:

TrueView Ads

TrueView Ads are the standards and most common ads that you see on YouTube videos. You pay for TrueView ads only when the viewer watches at least 30 seconds of the ad, or if they engage with it, for instance, with clicking on a call-to-action. These ads are skippable, which means that if the viewer is not interested in watching them, they can hit the **'Skip'** button on the right, choose not to watch the ad, and you will not pay a dime for that. These skippable ads can be anywhere from 12 seconds to 6 minutes long.

There are two parts of skippable TrueView ads:

#1: Video Discovery Ads

Video Discovery, or previously called In-Display Ads, are those ads that show on the video search result pages, YouTube homepage, and as videos that are related. Once the viewer clicks to watch the video, on the right, a display ad banner will appear.

#2: In-Stream Ads

In-Stream ads are those advertisements that appear within the video and play before the viewer even get the chance to watches the selected video. Usually, viewers have the chance to skip the ad after 5 seconds of playing, if they are not interested. These ads are great for marketers because they can be easily customized with the chance of including different call-to-action buttons.

Preroll Ads

Although technically they are non-skippable in-stream ads, the preroll ads are those ads that the viewers cannot skip, and that appear before, after, or even mid-roll videos. These preroll ads can be from 15-20 seconds long and are most successful if they are created with CTAs in order to optimize the viewer's attention that you have for these limited seconds. Your job here is to create a compelling ad that will encourage the viewers to click on the ad in order to receive something in return (like signing up for a demo product or some event).

Bumpers

The shortest type of ads on YouTube is called bumpers. They are only 6 seconds short and, to be honest, are not the best way to tell a story, however, if you are looking for a quick way to complement the launch of your new product or event, they can be of great value. Make sure to use these few seconds wisely and make sure to include only the elements that you want your viewers to actually remember.

<u>Creating Your Ad Campaign</u>

Once your marketing video is completed, the next step is to create the campaign in which you will advertise your clip on YouTube. To get started, go to Google AdWords account (sign up if you don't have one) and let's create the campaign:

Type – Click on the '**+ Campaign**' button and choose '**Video**' to choose the type of your campaign.

Name – Here, enter the name of your campaign.

Ad Format – Choose the format of your video ad. For instance, choose '**In-stream or video discovery ads**'.

Budget – Set how much money you wish to spend per day. Here, you can also select the method of delivery, meaning you can choose whether to show your video ads evenly during that day (standard delivery), or you can choose to drive views quickly (accelerated delivery).

Networks – You can choose where you want your video ads to appear. You have two options:

1. YouTube Videos: These ads will play before or mid-roll videos.

2. YouTube Search: Your ad will appear on the YouTube homepage, the video search

results, and listed in the related video column.

Make sure to create different campaigns for these two networks so you can measure the success separately and more effectively.

Locations – Filter the location of the users that you want the ad to be shown to, for instance, you can only choose California, United States. You also have the option to exclude some places as well.

Language, Device & Mobile Bidding – This is a great option that allows you to specify the device, mobile carrier, and operating system for a more successful targeting. You can also decrease or increase your bid if the video is shown on a mobile device.

Advanced Settings – In this section, you can set the start and end date of your campaign, limit the daily views, create a schedule for when the ad should be displayed, etc. This allows you to personalize your ad and get the most return.

Creating the Video Ad Creative – Once you name your ad group, you can also add the link to the YouTube video that you wish the ad to play for. Then, you will choose whether you wish to display the ad as an in-display or in-stream ad.

Bidding – Choose the maximum price that you want to pay for each ad view.

Targeting – Define your audience even further to ensure views from people who will want to be engaged with the ad. You can target by age, gender, location, interest, parental status, etc.

Advanced Targeting – Here, you can target your audience by relevant keywords or even websites that you want your ad to be shown.

Linking – Finally, if you haven't done it already, link your Google AdWord account to your YouTube channel, Click **'Finish'** and start your campaign.

Instagram

If you still think of Instagram as the social media platform where you post your selfies and well-plated restaurant foods, you need to change your opinion at this instant. Okay, I admit, that's what Instagram was when it first started in October 2010. But fast forward 8 and a half years later, and you see a platform that is filled with valuable tools for businesses. If you want to market your brand successfully online, then having a strong Instagram presence is definitely a must.

Instagram has over 800 million active monthly users, but statistics aside, the main reason why you should choose to learn this platform inside out and decide to have a marketing presence there, is the fact that Instagram users are not just active, they are engaged.

Instagram is all about the visual, and if you happen to be in the ecommerce business, well, marketing your brand on Instagram may just mean hitting the jackpot.

Setting Up Your Instagram Business Account

In order for you to set up your Instagram business page, you first need to have an Instagram account up and running. To do so, you will have to have the Instagram app downloaded.

When you open the app, you will see two options: to log in with Facebook, or to sign up with an Email or Phone. Make sure to use a business email for this purpose to make sure that your Instagram profile will not be linked to your personal Facebook account.

After that, enter your details. Under **Full Name**, enter the name of your business, and under **Username**, write down the unique name for your Instagram profile that will be recognizable so that people can easily find it and engage with the content.

Next, add a profile picture for your Instagram profile. Whether a logo or a photo of your store, the main point is for the picture to be clear and distinctive.

Now that you have an Instagram account, the next step is to make it a business one. In order for your account to be a business account, it will have to be linked with a Facebook business page. Assuming that you have already taken care of that, open your Instagram profile. Tap on the **'Settings'** icon in the upper right corner. Once there, go to **'Switch to Business Profile'** → **'Continue'** to connect with your Facebook page. Keep in mind that your profile will need to be set to public, so make sure that the 'Private' option is not selected.

There, you should see your Facebook page as an option. Select it and click on **'Continue As'.** Tap **'Next'**.

Once you're all set, you will be prompted to enter some company info such as address, phone number, and email address. This is important for your customers to get in touch with you, so make sure to enter valid information. Click **'Done'** and that's it.

Optimizing Your Profile

Congratulations! Now you are a proud owner of an Instagram business account. But wait before thinking you've got what it takes to jump straight to posting your content. There are a couple more steps that need to be taken care of in order for your profile to look professional and, most importantly, attractive to your audience.

As mentioned before, Instagram is all about the visual. That means that it should be a good reflection of your brand, but at the same time, it should also provide a constant aesthetic look.

The Color Scheme

Your Instagram color scheme should be consistent and have a sort of a flow. The colors should go together seamlessly and it should give away a good feeling, whatever you go for the dark and cold or the bright and warm feed.

The Lighting

Just as the color, the lighting is also a crucial element for the aesthetic. If not sure what I mean, think about your favorite magazine for a second. Whatever the subject there, the good lighting is what keeps everything together and provides an elegant look.

Evenly Spaced-Out Content

To keep your Instagram profile visually appealing, besides lighting and coloring, the way your photos are spaced out is also an important ingredient. The main thing is that your feed should blend together. Try not to clump together a lot of busy photos, but find a balance between them and the minimal ones for a beautiful and attractive look.

Have Consistent Editing

Another important thing you need to have in mind before you actually start uploading the photos, is that they need to have a consistent editing style. You don't need to use only one filter, of course, but try to have a more cohesive look by keeping the style the same so that your photos will flow.

Writing Your Bio

The Instagram bio is by far the most under-utilized part of Instagram profiles, but that doesn't mean that it's not important. Quite the opposite, actually. If you are a business that wants to promote its products or services on Instagram, then having an eye-catching bio that will introduce your brand to customers is so much more than just an option.

But simply writing your name, website, and address will not do the trick. You will need to actually write down what your business is and what you do in a shortly descriptive and equally creative way. This is the time to stand out and let people know what makes your brand better than other similar ones. If you have a certain tool or service that makes you stand out, include that in your info.

Another thing you need to include in your bio is *#hashtags.* Thanks to an update that happened in

2018, your profile username and hashtags from your bio are now clickable links. By including '#' and '@' before the words, they will become a hyperlink that will take your audience to another page. Pretty beneficial for promoting your brand, right?

Once you've set everything up, take one final look and see if you're satisfied with the way you have introduced your brand to the world.

Types of Insta Posts

If all looks good, it's time to post your content on Instagram. But before you do that, let's take a look at the different types of posts that you can share on your Instagram profile:

Images

The most popular type of post on Instagram is the image post. Keep in mind that when posting your brand's images on Instagram, it is important to share a variety of them. That way you will show your bra--nd's diversity and also help your audience engage with your content in many ways.

Another thing you need to understand when posting images, is that your audience (especially Instagram audience) is looking for genuine photos, not sales pitches and advertisements. Then how to promote your products, you may think. Try to focus on delivering a real-life message, not on sharing product images only. For instance, if you are selling clothes, instead of taking a photo of your newest shirt, try to post a photo of a model wearing that shirt with beautiful scenery in the background.

Behind-the-Scenes Posts

This is probably the type of post that is appreciated the most. Posting from behind the scenes allows your audience to take a look at how things are done in your company and get a feel of the atmosphere there. For instance, you can share a photo that will show your employees at work on a busy day.

The key to these posts is realness. The post needs to look authentic and not staged in order to attract your customer's eye.

Reposts from Employees

Looking for an original way to post? How about reposting some great content that your employees have already shared? Reposting images from the Instagram profiles of your employees (and tagging them, of course) is a great way to make your brand seem a bit more 'human' and enhance the originality of your profile. This way you will show your audience that your team has a special bond, which will encourage them to engage.

Motivational Posts

Motivational posts include simple images with a quote or other uplifting and motivational text. But as much as these posts can help you increase the value of your brand, if not executed tastefully, they will sound cheesy and fake. Taste them sparingly to look more original.

Influencer Posts

Influencer posts are those posts that are shared by a celebrity or another well-known person who has a massive fan base. For instance, if you sell healthy and organic drinks, you may want to choose to contact an athlete or a famous wellness coach to post a picture of them drinking one of your smoothies. The point here is to extend your audience and reach some of the influencer's fans. How to do it? Find and contact an influencer with the inquiry, offering something in return. Many of them will do it for free samples, but others may ask money in return.

Educational Posts

Those posts that offer quick tips on how to make or do something are called educational posts. They can either be videos or photos, but the main thing is that they offer simple instructions that the audience can follow in order to achieve something.

User-Generated Content

If reposts from employees meant sharing images and videos that your employees have posted, user-generated content means curating posts that have been shared by your followers. Deciding to share a post from a customer will not only make their day, but it will also show your other followers that you truly care for your customers. Just make sure to credit the original image or video and tag the poster.

Newsjacking

Newsjacking means trending holiday posts. But I do not only mean the huge holidays such as Christmas or Valentine's Day. There is a holiday for pretty much everything, so you might want to consider getting into its spirit and share upbeat messages for these carefree moments.

TAKING QUALITY IMAGES

Now that you've learned what kind of images you can share on Instagram, let's see how to actually post appealing ones that will draw the attention of your audience and make them hit the 'like' button and comment.

First of all, follow the rules for the image size:

Square Images – 1080 x 1080 pixels

Landscape Images – 1080 x 566 pixels

Profile Images – 1350 x 1080 pixels

The Rule of Thirds

Moving the subject from the center and creating an imbalance of the photo is a very popular and appealing technique that most photographers love to use. Called the rule of the thirds, this technique will be loved by your followers.

For convenient photo taking, make sure that the grid lines on your smartphone are turned on.

Single Subject Is the Key

Posting chaotic photos will not catch your follower's eye, as simple and organized ones will.

Try to focus on a single subject when shooting photos. That means cropping out and getting rid of unnecessary things in the frame, making the extra subject blurry, or shooting against a simple and clear background.

Say Yes to the Negative Space

Negative space is a term for the empty space that is around your subject. In terms of promoting a single product, shooting with a lot of negative space is just the thing you need. That way, your follower's eye will be drawn right where you want it to be – on your product.

Take Advantage of Different Perspective

We people see the world around us from an eye level. For that purpose, professional photographers, usually, take photos from a different perspective and use various angles, to make the image seem as realistic as possible.

Play with Patterns and Symmetry

137

Whether a wooden table or a tiled floor, choose an attractive pattern that will be disrupted by your subject. Try to break the rule of thirds from time to time, and add some symmetry to your photos by placing your subject in the middle of your chosen pattern.

Natural Light is Your Friend

Natural light works best in photography. Try not to overshadow your subject by standing overhead your lighting, but tend to take advantage of the natural light by shooting outdoors or next to a window.

Videos

As long as the video is 60 seconds or less long, it can be uploaded on Instagram.

Boomerangs

Boomerang is an Instagram setting that allows you to take 3-second videos that can play both, forwards and backwards. By tapping the camera icon on Instagram and choosing the **'Boomerang'** setting, you can easily upload a Boomerang to Instagram. Boomerangs are a fun way to showcase upbeat circumstances such as jumping or high-fiving.

You can also create a Boomerang by combining photos for a repetitive and entertaining video.

Hyperlapse

Hyperlapse for Instagram is a tool that will allow you to cut your long videos short and transform them into content that can be posted on Instagram. Download the app Hyperlapse and you can record your own time lapse videos, save, and upload.

Instagram Live

Just like Facebook Live, Instagram also offers the option to share live content. If you are interested in engaging with your customers this way, just open your Instagram camera, choose the **'Live'** setting, and then simply hit the **'Start Live Video'** button. Once you start your live video stream, all of your followers who are online at the moment, will receive a notification. Your live audience can also engage real-time by commenting on your live video, which is a great opportunity for a real-time Q&A session with your customers.

IGTV

IGTV or Instagram TV is the most recent video feature by Instagram. This is a way for Instagram users to watch longer vertical videos, which can also be great for your marketing strategy if you were thinking about including some longer explainer videos or even some interviews.

IGTV can be accessed either through the Instagram app, or through its own IGTV app that can be downloaded from your App Store. If you are thinking about posting on IGTV though, you will have to download the app and create a channel there. After that, you can upload videos that are anywhere from 15 seconds to 10 minutes in length. If you have a verified account you can run your videos for up to an hour. You can only use IGTV on your smartphone, as this platform cannot be accessed through your desktop computer yet.

Keep in mind that this is not the same as Instagram Live. IGTV is previously recorded and uploaded footage, which gives you the opportunity to fine-tune and edit your video for as long as you'd like.

Instagram Stories

Instagram stories is a very popular feature on Instagram that is basically, a solution to over-posting. It is basically a way for you to post on Instagram frequently, but without polluting your main feed.

This is a time-sensitive feature that shows a bit rawer look, unlike your filtered photos. It is much more authentic than your usual posts, which is why it is deeply appreciated by the followers.

There are three ways in which you can post your Instagram Story:

1. Tap the camera icon in the top left corner

2. Type the **'Your Story +'** found above your feed

3. Or simply swipe right with your finger to open your camera

Your story can also be filtered or doodled on. You can also add text or even include a GIF, music, add a location, and a ton of other fun features. And the best part? Instagram actually allows you to tag another Instagram account in your Story, so that is a cool way to connect with a similar business, a team member, or you can also use this feature to personally tag a customer to thank for the support.

To publish, just press the **'Your Story +'** button, or you can simply choose to save for later and post the story when it is more convenient for you. You can find your story at the top of your main feed and also through your profile picture.

Writing Eye-Catching Captions

Although it is the picture that first catches the viewer's eye, if the caption underneath it is less than remarkable, your audience will not be tempted to engage with it. But how to write outstanding captions? Follow these simple tips below to avoid getting overwhelmed with finding the right words.

Take Your Time

Okay, you are not writing a chapter for your novel. You don't actually need days to brainstorm the perfect line that will accompany your new picture, but writing a couple of drafts and asking the opinion of your friends and family can surely help. The main purpose of your posts is to be engaging to users, especially with the new Instagram algorithm. When users visit the Instagram app, the top posts that they see are the ones that Instagram thinks they will find to be the most engaging. That should be a good reason for you to find the time to craft captions that will wow your audience.

The Beginning Counts the Most

Instagram allows 2,200 characters in the captions, which is a great thing if you are comparing this platform with Twitter where you cannot post more than 140 characters. However, keep in mind that your audience will not see the whole text on their screens. It is only the first couple of lines that are shown; to read the rest of the text, your audience needs to click the 'More' button. If you really want to tell a story that people will actually read, make the first few lines as attention-grabbing as possible, to get your customers hooked. There is no reason for you to shy away from getting into details and writing longer captions, as long as you write killer beginnings. However, if you want your audience to do most of the talking, then shorter captions work best.

Engage!

It seems I cannot stress this enough, but ENGAGEMENT really is the key to successful marketing. Otherwise, you are just another brand selling unimportant stuff to people. To encourage your audience to engage, make sure to <u>always</u> include a call-to-action in your captions and ask your audience to like, share, and comment on your post.

Work on Your Instagram Voice

Remember how we said that you need to have a separate approach for every platform? Your voice should be different for each of your social media profiles. What promotes your brand on LinkedIn will probably not work for Instagram. Your posts on Instagram should be carefree, upbeat, and written with a unique tone that will become recognizable for your brand over time. Give your brand a distinct feel by playing with words, colors, emojis, and other creative tools.

Their Majesty, the #Hashtags

Unless you are new to social media and not that present on the internet, then you probably already know what hashtags are. They are the keyword phrases that are spelled together, without spaces, and have the '#' sign standing proudly before them. Although they were born on Twitter, hashtags have now completely taken over social media.

Why should you use hashtags? Because they will help your content get noticed, and when you take into consideration that Instagram has over 80 million photos shared every day, you see how that's useful, right? Get it right, and your audience will engage in no time.

There are three ways in which your audience can see tagged content on Instagram:

1. First, they see their TOP 9 posts, which are tagged posts that Instagram thinks the user will most likely want to engage with

2. The most RECENT 9 posts, which shows tagged posts displayed in chronological order

3. RELATED hashtags, which displays similar hashtags that people use to discuss that or a related topic.

To make sure that you can broaden the reach of your post, use a few extra hashtags that are related and that will help your audience notice the photo. For instance, if you want to tag your photo with #smoothie, you may want to add hashtags like

#vegan, #healthysnack, or #matchapowder. The point is to tag a few extra details that will explain the subject of your photo.

Note: Your account must be PUBLIC in order for your tagged posts to be displayed on the hashtag feeds.

Finding the Right Hashtag

But what if you cannot decide on which hashtags to use? That can also be easily solved, as finding hashtags within the Instagram app is actually the simplest way. Have a hashtag in mind? Just type your preferred hashtag into the 'Search Bar' of Instagram, filter your search results by Tags, and see how many posts have actually used that hashtag, see related hashtags, and brainstorm some relevant keyword phrases.

Want to increase your reach? Why not throw some trending hashtags into your post and combine them with your specific keywords to make the post more relevant?

Formatting Your Hashtag

Now that you've found the perfect hashtags for your post, you need to decide how to actually use them. The main rule here is to be natural. The used hashtags should have a flow and go well together. Read your post out loud before pressing 'Share' and see how it feels. Sounds kind of spammy? Don't worry! Even if your hashtags cannot be incorporated into the post as you want them to, you can always choose to place them at the end of your post, or even in the beginning. They'll do the same job regardless of their place.

Note: Businesses use an average of 2.5 hashtags per post. Try to limit your hashtags and never include more than 4, to avoid seeming like you try too hard in order to keep your audience interested.

Marketing Your Brand

The biggest mistake you can possibly make is to approach Instagram without a decent marketing strategy in mind. Posting high-quality content with the perfect hashtags will not be enough if you don't have a perfectly crafted strategy. Being a unique social media platform, Instagram requires its own distinctive way of promoting. Read on to see what you can do to help your brand grow with this platform.

Know Your Audience

Knowing exactly who your audience is, is the only way to ensure that you are promoting your brand to the right people and expect engagement in return. If you are already marketing your products on other social media platform, you can use that audience, but keep in mind that Instagram audience is a bit different.

To find your perfect Instagram audience, spend some time monitoring the hashtags that are related to your brand and the products/services you are selling. Check out the people who are using these hashtags, and take a look at their profiles. Take notes of the factors that define your perfect buyer persona and create your perfect audience.

149

Analyze!

You are just starting out your Instagram marketing journey, which means that you cannot be exactly sure what works and what is not s appreciated by the audience. To get a clear picture of what posts get the highest engagement and what photos sit forgotten, spend some time peeking into your competitors' profiles. See their performance and take notes of the things that have managed to engage the audience the most. After all, wasn't it Picasso who said that great artists steal? I am not talking about copyright infringement, of course, but use their profiles as a guidance of what and when to share to connect with your followers.

Post When Your Audience is Active the Most

If you type "what is the best time to post on Instagram" on Google, you will find a number of websites all showing recent statistics based on millions of posts and user engagement. In fact, the most recent ones say that the best time to share your content is between 9 and 11 am EST. But that does not mean that that's the time when YOUR brand's audience is most active.

There are many ways in which you can find the perfect time to post for your business. Monitoring your audience and taking notes on when different time zones are the most active, as well as tracking your posts' progress over time are both great gauges. But, if you are looking for the most hassle-free option, then downloading some algorithms that will automatically calculate this for you is probably the best choice.

If you don't like any of these options, then sticking to the rule of 9am-11am can also be productive. Also, consider other factors that are important for your business as well. For instance, if your audience is made of teenagers and young adults, then avoid posting early in the morning.

Schedule Your Posts

Once you find out what the perfect time for posting is for your business, make sure to actually share your posts then. The best way to ensure that the post will not slip your mind and will actually be shared at the right time, is to schedule it.

Simply, write down your post and open the drop-down menu found at the bottom of your screen. There, choose **'Publish on Scheduled Date'**, select the preferred date and time, and wait for Instagram to take care of the rest for you. If you are too busy, you can also use a scheduling tool for this purpose where you can write a couple of posts in advance and schedule the date and time when you want them to be published. www.sendible.com and www.later.com both include great management tools for your Instagram profile.

Be Consistent!

Although we have already mentioned this, consistency really is the key. In order for it to be successful, your brand first needs to be consistent on Instagram. And I do not mean only with the posts. Consistency should run all over your feed, from the colors of your profile to how your photos are organized. Knowing what your brand's personality is and adjusting your content to match it, is the best way to catch some eyes and attract new followers.

Attracting Followers

Although every single one of the previously mentioned techniques will help you attract followers on Instagram, there are a couple of tricks that you need to have up your sleeve in order to increase your fan base and get some more likes.

Become a Follower

Assuming that your name and bio are written in a compelling manner, that your profile is optimized as discussed before, and that you've already started posting quality content, the next thing you need to do is start following accounts. Following similar accounts and some other interests that are related to your business will help you become a part of a community that might throw many followers your way. Once you start following people and businesses, Instagram will also suggest other related accounts that you can become a fan of.

But don't let that end there. When you become their follower, start interacting with their content. That will not only spread awareness of your brand, but it will also humanize it, which people greatly appreciate.

Ask for Interaction

Asking people to spread the word is a great marketing strategy that might require some more work, but always pays out. Start with your friends and family and get them to share your account and ask their followers to become your followers. Get in touch with brand ambassadors and kindly ask them to share the content you post with other similar accounts that might help you increase your follower list. Just try not to be pushy and always give something in return. Free samples and generous discounts always seem to do the trick.

Partnering up with an influencer can be pretty valuable. By having the influencer promoting your products, you can 'borrow' some of their followers and drive more traffic to your account.

Go with Instagram Stories

Take advantage of Instagram Stories for more exposure of your brand. How? Besides being a great tool that will help you connect your already existing audience, Instagram Stories can also increase your list of followers, thanks to the fact that they appear on the Instagram Search page. That means that even if someone is not your follower, they can still find your Instagram Stories from the Explore page when searching for something similar.

Promote

Just like with Facebook and YouTube, promoting your Instagram profile on your website and other social media platforms, is the simplest, but sometimes the easiest way to attract new followers that will become your fans on Instagram.

Turning Followers into Customers

Having a lot of Instagram followers can be great for your business. But if those people simply click the 'Follow' button and your connection with them ends there, then your marketing strategy will, most likely, go up in smoke. The key isn't to gather as many followers as possible but to actually turn them into customers. Here are some things that can help you encourage your followers to take some action:

Promotions. People on Instagram love promotions and first-time sales. Limited deals and special offerings can attract your followers to give your brand a chance and see what you are selling. Just remember to emphasize the importance of fast action and mention a fixed deadline so your followers can take the plunge as soon as possible.

Charity. Looking for a way to attract more millennials? How about setting aside some of your profit and donating it to a charity? Studies show that more than 80 % of the millennials expect companies to make generous donations, so try to live up to their expectations. Besides building compassion for your brand, that way you can also get your followers to get involved and support a really important cause. That might turn them into long-term customers of yours.

Contests. Contests are the perfect way to get people to try out your products. Make it a requirement for people to follow your account or even make a post by tagging your brand in order to enter the contest.

Teasers. Posting teasers of your new products is the perfect way to let your audience have a quick look at what you are working on. Combine your teasers with limited promotions and let people purchase your hot, new product for a special price.

Live Launches. Instagram Live offers a great opportunity for you to launch your new products live. This will encourage your customers to get

157

engaged, since this option offers a chance for them to ask you some questions about the product in real time.

What About Analytics?

I hate to disappoint you, but Instagram doesn't have an analytics tool like the built-in ones that Facebook and YouTube offer. Fingers crossed, this will soon be changed for the better. However, that doesn't mean that you cannot track your Instagram success. Below you will find some tips that will help you measure your brand's growth on Instagram and get a clear picture of your business' performance.

First of all, once you switch to a Business account, Instagram does offer some limited tools such as measuring the growth of your followers, their engagement, the organic reach, etc. You can access this tool by clicking on the **'View Insights'** button that's found just below your photos and videos.

If you are looking for a more in-depth way to track your Instagram metrics, then purchasing a third-party tool that will allow you to measure your performance more effectively is probably a good choice. https://pro.iconosquare.com/ is a great management tool for that purpose. Their pricing varies from 29 euros to 79 euros per month, depending on your plan and commitment, but the best part is that they offer a 14-day free trial for you to see what they can do for your marketing strategy and decide whether they are worth the investment.

You can also go to your Facebook's Ad Manager for some Instagram metrics, but keep in mind that this option is pretty limited and it is not for every post or campaign.

Advertising on Instagram

Once you become active on Instagram, you need to consider investing in advertising your content there in order to increase your traffic and get more shares. If you are familiar with Facebook advertising then you have already halfway through

Instagram marketing, as the setup and budgeting for your Insta ads are actually done through Facebook.

To begin the process, your Instagram Business account must be claimed and linked to your Facebook Page.

Once you take care of that, choose your editor of choice (Ads Manager, Facebook Ads API or Power Editor). The Ads Manager is the most popular with social media marketers, so you might want to choose that tool.

The next step is selecting the objective for your ad. You will see that there are quite a few options, but for Instagram advertising, these are the ones that you need to choose from:

- Brand Awareness

- Engagement

- Reach

- Traffic

- Conversions

- App Installs

- Video Views

Then, name your ad set, and target your audience. You will be given a few factors to set, such as age, location, gender, behavior, work, etc. Or, if you have one, you can also choose a previously-created custom audience.

Then, choose the **'Edit Placement'** option and click on **'Instagram'** under the given platforms. This is a very important step because if you do not choose Instagram, you will only advertise on Facebook.

Next, you will be asked to set your budget and schedule your ads. As discussed earlier, complete this step and move forward to setting up your content. There are two options for you here, you can either choose to boost an existing post, or you can upload a new photo or video to run as an advertisement.

161

Once everything is set, simply click on the **'Place Order'** button and that's it. Your Instagram ad campaign is ready to run. Just be sure to report on your performance and keep a track of the ad progress. You can find the metrics for this purpose either in the Facebook Ads Manager or in your marketing software, in case you are using one.

Twitter

With approximately 6,000 new tweets per second, Twitter is definitely a great platform for your business. Whatever your goals may be, chances are, a huge chunk of the 326 million of monthly active Twitter users represent your target audience. With that in mind, it is safe to say that marketing your brand on Twitter can turn out to be a very profitable strategy for you. But simply signing up and tweeting will not be enough. Just like with any other social media platform, you also need a well-crafted marketing strategy for Twitter. This chapter will help you learn how to promote your brand on Twitter and discover the possibilities hiding behind Larry the bird.

How is Twitter Different?

We already talked about the importance of having a different approach to your social media channels. What works for Facebook may not work for your Twitter profile. But when it comes to social media platforms, Twitter really is the one that stands out.

Unlike Instagram or Pinterest, Twitter does not put the emphasis on broadcasting content. Instead, Twitter is all about the conversation and communication between users, whether ordinary people, companies or even government officials.

The top reasons why businesses mostly use Twitter are:

- Sharing information

- Branding

- Driving engagement

- Interacting with customers

- Reputation management

- Networking

Twitter is the platform that thrives off the interaction. That's how it is different. Because it is not a platform that has consumption and distribution of content as a main purpose. On Twitter, people usually go to become a part of an interaction and engage with the content, not to watch videos or scroll through photos.

Creating Your Twitter Profile

If you're just a person who's interested in what the world's leaders have to say next, sure, you can just sign up, upload a photo (or not), and start retweeting. But if you are a business and want to market your brand on Twitter, then an in-depth and carefully-created profile is indeed required.

Follow these next few steps to create a Twitter account for your business:

1. Go to www.twitter.com.

2. Click on the **'Sign Up'** button.

3. Enter the required information and then hit **'Create my account'.**

4. When you click **'Next'** on your homepage, Twitter will ask you to follow 5 people. Make sure that they are related to your business in some way.

165

5. You can choose to add contacts from your email address at this point, but this step is optional. Your Twitter account is now created.

Go to your profile and click on **'Edit Profile'**. The first thing you need to do is upload your profile picture, which for business is usually their logo or some other photo that represent their brand.

The Bio

Unfortunately, you only get 160 characters to introduce your business to the Twitter world. On the plus side, this gives you an opportunity to get really creative, carefully select your words, and say only the things that matter the most.

Just like on Facebook, YouTube, and Instagram, your brand's bio on Twitter should also include relevant keywords that will help your customer discover you better. Keep in mind that it should be enticing, upbeat and attract followers. It seems that fun bios work like a magnet for the audience, so you might want to add a humorous line to catch some more eyes.

The Optimization

Your bio is important, but if your whole profile is not strategically optimized, then humorous lines and relevant keywords will not do the trick. Your profile should be able not only to visually attract potential customers, but also to encourage them to actually start a conversation about the products or services that you are selling.

Add a professional profile picture that represents your brand (like your logo or a storefront) and upload a high-quality header image that will complement the profile picture; think an upcoming event or the newest product.

Once your exterior is pleasant to the eye, take advantage of hashtags and emojis, and make sure to post content that your audience will find valuable.

The Verification

Getting verified on Twitter is an important part. A verified profile means that you are the real deal and that your audience can trust you. Having the blue checkmark next to your account name can be of great value for your business, so make sure that you verify your profile right from the start.

Let People Know

Know that your profile is not only up and running, but optimized for success as well, it is time to show it off. Whether on your website, other social media platforms, email signature, or added on the front window of your store, letting people know about your Twitter handle is the best strategy for boosting your list of followers.

The Right Marketing Strategy

Marketing your brand on Twitter goes way beyond setting up your profile the right way. It is the proper mix of activities that will boost the process of promoting your brand, and in turn, bring you more customers. But to do so, these marketing-oriented activities must be planned for and carefully designed. Here is how you can power-pack the process of marketing your brand on Twitter:

Listen and Take Notes

When people think of marketing (whether on social media or not), they usually have investing money in mind. And while it is true that the more you invest, the higher the chances for returns, when it comes to promoting your brand, the crucial strategy is often glossed over. The first step, before reaching for your wallet, is to see exactly where you (and your competition) stand. And since we are talking about Twitter marketing, the first step is to check just how engaged are people with your brand.

The very first thing you need to tackle, is to check what the community on Twitter is talking about your brand. What are people interested in the most? What do they think you should improve? What are they not satisfied with? Knowing this can help you crush the competitors and get instant feedback from your customers.

Here are some things that you need to listen for on Twitter:

- The name of your brand

- The name of your products and services

- Your competition

- Your brand's slogans

- Some buzzword in your industry

- The name of your CEO or some other representatives

- Campaign names

- Other important keywords

Take notes of the things that are relevant for your brand and incorporate in your other marketing activities in order to have more satisfied customers.

Create Great Content

This goes without saying, but posting great content is usually what hooks the audience, makes them retweet, share, and engage with your brand. You have only 280 characters, so you should be picky with your words, and say only the things that are the most relevant for your brand and that are highly likely to resonate with your Twitter audience.

Be Helpful. Besides listening to what they have to say or engaging with them directly, it is great to actually show your audience that you care about their needs and interests by helping them in some way. Sharing a trending content that your audience will find helpful is a great way to become more appreciated by your customers. If you don't know how to find one, visit download the *'TrendSpottr'* app and discover some emerging trends.

Use #Hashtags. Ok, I've said this too many times, but hashtags are the single most important thing when it comes to Twitter marketing. Without them, you may as well be writing in your notebook, not sharing your content online. Why? Because it is the hashtags that make sure that your content will be actually discovered and seen by people.

Be Conversational. Making Twitter one-dimensional is a social-media marketing crime. Your Tweets shouldn't be sole broadcasts, but have to open the door for interaction and conversation:

- Ask your audience questions

- Make sure that at least 30 percent of your Tweets are replies

- Do not Tweet mere links; make sure to include a line of your own thoughts, as well

- Make sure to Tweet out directly to your audience

Plan Ahead

You should always be active. That means that for every holiday and special event, you need to get into the spirit. When late November rolls around, you should start with your Christmas tweets. Come mid-January, your Valentine's tweets need to be decorating your Twitter profile. Be in touch with the latest trends, and do not forget to use the right #Holiday hashtags.

Post at the Right Time

Tweets do not last forever. Just because you talked about something ten days ago, does not mean that, when your audience decides that it is time to address the issue, they will engage with your content. It is important to know what the right time to post is in order to be in the middle of the conversation.

Tweet Regularly. Tweeting once a day is a great way to stay active and participate in the hottest conversations. You can try to post more than that, but keep your eyes open and see how that will affect your Twitter presence. That way, you can find the frequency that works best for your brand.

Stick to the Best Practice. It is said that the best times to post on Twitter are 12 pm, 5 pm, and 6 pm. Of course, this depends on your audience, so experimenting and measuring here is, again, recommended in order to find what suits you the most.

Schedule Your Tweets. Once you determine the best times to share your content, schedule your Tweets to ensure that you will get the most engagement for each of your Tweets. https://hootsuite.com/ is a great tool that can help you with scheduling your Tweets.

Twitter Video

Although Twitter is not the first thing that comes to mind when thinking about promoting your brand through video content, statistics say that the Twitter community is very much interested in digesting videos, as well.

There are a few options available when it comes to sharing videos via Twitter:7

1. First, you can use the native feature on Twitter that allows you to record up to 140 seconds and upload directly.

174

2. Another option is to use a live streaming app called Periscope (owned by Twitter) which integrates into your profile and makes sure that your live stream will be seen by your followers. Once you are done recording, the stream will become available to your audience.

Thread Tweets Together

Want to provide content in an even more organized matter? Try threading tweets together. This facility allows you to start a tweet and then continue adding more tweets to the original one, by simply threading them to the first tweet. This is a great way to tell a story or keep an ongoing conversation alive, without having content all over the place.

Measuring the Results

Measuring what your marketing strategy has achieved so far is the best way to evaluate your Twitter success and determine just how much your audience is engaged with your brand. This simple activity can help you pinpoint your weak spots, as well as your strengths, and help you determine how you should change the strategy and what is worth investing in.

Twitter Analytics

Twitter Analytics is the built-in tool for tracking the overall performance of your Twitter account. To use Twitter Analytics, click on your avatar and then select the **'Analytics'** in order to see your month-by-month highlights. You can also jump straight to analytics.twitter.com.

There you will find:

Top Tweet – The tweet that has earned the most impressions for a selected month.

New Followers – The number of people that have clicked the 'Follow' button for the given month.

Top Follower – This represents the person who has the most followers (out of your New Followers).

Top Mention – A tweet where a user mentions your brand that has earned the most impressions for that month.

Engagements – Anything that users click on (photos, links, videos, likes, etc,)

Engagement Rate – Once you divide the number of engagements by the number of impressions for a certain tweet, you get the engagement rate.

Reach Percentage – It's calculated by dividing the number of tweet impressions by the total number of followers, and it shows how many followers saw the selected tweet.

Other great tools that Twitter Analytics offer are **'Audiences'** – where you can gather intel on your audience (location, gender, interests, etc.) and **'Ad Campaign Dashboard'** – where you will gain access to the performance of your active promotions.

Advertising on Twitter

If you want to keep your Tweets from getting lost in the whirlpool of active content, then giving them a little boost to make sure that they will be seen by your audience, seems like the smart thing to do. Twitter ads can help you get the message to the right customers.

Type of Twitter Ads

There are a couple of ways in which you can promote on Twitter:

Promoted Tweets

These are tweets that you pay to make sure that people who are not already following you Twitter will see. Just like with regular tweets, the promoted tweets can also be liked, retweeted, shared, etc. The only difference between them and the regular tweets is in the **'Promoted'** sign next to them.

Promoted Accounts

Promoted accounts do not promote your Tweets but your Twitter profile. They help your account get discovered more and bring you more followers, by promoting your Tweeter profile to people who may be interested in your brand, but are not already following you.

Promoted Trends

Trends are those subjects on Twitter that people talk about the most. Promoted trends is an option that allows you to promote your own #hashtag at the top of the list of the most popular trends. So, when Twitter users search for a specific trend, they will see a list of organic results, with your hashtag at the top. This will gain you more organic exposure and enhance your list of followers.

Automated Ads

Although customized Twitter ads are a better way to reach your specific business goal, there is another option for those that are unsure of how much they want to spend, have a limited time, or lack the strong team. That option is called *Twitter Promoted Mode*.

Twitter Promoted Mode are automated ads that you pay a flat fee for. With a fixed price of $99 (plus tax) per month, you can have your first 10 tweets (of the day) promoted to your target audience, automatically.

According to Twitter, you can expect to reach about 30,000 people with this option. Also, this will most likely get you approximately 30 new followers each month.

Creating Your Ad Campaign

Creating a Twitter ads campaign is a very straight forward process. Just follow the steps below and your Tweets are ready to be promoted.

#1: The Ads Account

If it is your first time using Twitter for advertising, you will need to have an account. Visit https://ads.twitter.com/login to get started.

#2: The Objective

Your ad campaign must be based on a specific objective for your business, meaning that this is the step where you decide what it is that you want to achieve with your Twitter ads. Whether it is to reach more followers, build your brand's awareness, increase the engagement rate or another reason, choose your objective wisely and click **'Next'** to continue.

#3: The Ad Group and Bidding

At this point, you choose your ad-group, which is a sub category of your campaign. At this point, it is recommended to stick to a single ad-group, but as you become more comfortable with Twitter advertising, you can split it into a couple sub-groups to target different audiences or experiment with budgets and timing.

Here, you will also have to choose your budget, or how much you want to pay for every interaction (video view, engagement, etc.)

When you're all set, click **'Next'** for the next step.

#4: The Creative and Ad Placement

Select the tweet you want to promote from a list of old tweets, or simply create a new one here. Then, choose the ad placement:

- Users' timelines

- Profiles and Tweet detail pages

- Search results

Again, click **'Next'**.

#5: The Target Audience

Here, you need to go through several targeting options to select your preferred audience. You will have to select location, gender, age, language, technology, etc. in order to define the type of audience you want to promote your Tweets too. Also, you have the option to upload your own list of target audience (such as your email list), or you can also choose to target users that are similar to the audience who is already following you.

#6: The Launch

When you are all done, just click on **'Launch Campaign'** to start your campaign and launch your ads. And that's it.

LinkedIn

LinkedIn is the largest and most popular professional network with over 562 million users from all over the world. If you want to build your connections and expand your network, then being active on LinkedIn is an absolute must for your business. It is, after all, the top social network for lead generation.

Being a platform that connects companies and professionals, LinkedIn, most certainly, requires a unique marketing strategy. Here, the rule is the word of mouth. It is not about who you know, but about who can connect with through the people you know. But promoting your brand via your outdated personal page will not turn out to be a successful marketing plan. Read on to see how to create (and implement) your killer marketing strategy that will raise you to the top on LinkedIn.

Setting Up Your LinkedIn Company Page

To promote your brand on LinkedIn, you need a full-blown company page. The company page is a professional way to let LinkedIn users learn about your brand, your products, your company, as well as job opportunities that your company offers.

Although the company pages were primarily used as HR landing pages, now, this platform offers a great opportunity for increasing brand awareness and promoting your services to potential customers.

In order to set up a company page, you need an active LinkedIn personal profile first. Assuming that you have one, simply follow the next steps to create the page for your company.

Step #1: Add Your Company

Go to https://business.linkedin.com/marketing-solutions/linkedin-pages and click on **'Create Your Page'**. Enter the name of your company and come up with a URL that will help people find your page.

Note that you cannot change the URL later, so make sure to choose wisely. Then, check the checkbox to verify that you are an official representative of the company and click on **'Create Page'**.

The shell is automatically created. To start building your page, just click on the **'Get Started'** button.

Step #2: Add Your Image

Upload your logo (300 x 300 pixels recommended) as your profile picture, and add a cover image (preferably 1536 x 768 px) to offer a glimpse of what your company is about. Keep in mind that companies with logos have more traffic, so do not be tempted to skip this step.

Step #3: Create Your Description

LinkedIn allows you to use 2,000 characters for your description, but be aware that it is the first 156 words that appear in your company page's preview that is displayed on Google, so make sure to write an outstanding beginning.

You have the option to add 20 specialties. Think of them as keywords ad they can help people discover your company on LinkedIn, so make sure to represents the strength and expertise of your business here.

Step #4: Your Company's Details

Here, you will enter the location of your company, your website's URL, your industry, size and type of your company, as well as other important details that describe your business.

Step #5: Publish the Page

To go live, click on **'Publish'**. Before you continue, it is recommended to check what the company page looks like when other users click on it. To check it out, click on **'Member View'**. If you are not satisfied the look of your page, go to **'Manage Page'** and make some changes.

Step #6: Page Administrators

If you are not planning to run your LinkedIn company page alone, then you will have to choose the people that can administer the page.

To add more employees, click on the **'Me'** button found at the top of your page. Then, go to **'Manage'**, choose your Company Page. There, choose **'Admin Tools'** → **'Page Admins'**. Then, enter the name of the people you want to give access to the page.

Note: You have to already be connected to these people on LinkedIn in order to select them as administrators.

The Perfect Strategy

Simply creating a company page doesn't mean that the right connections will come your way. Just like with any other platform, you need to have a good marketing strategy for LinkedIn as well. Here is what you can do in order to enhance your chance for success:

Create a Showcase Page

Showcase pages are the perfect way to showcase a specific part of your company that you are most proud of. This is a great opportunity to put the spotlight on your best product and attract potential customers.

The showcase pages work as some sort of subdomains for your company page, and having one can really make a difference as LinkedIn users can also follow them separately if they are specifically interested in a particular product or service. You can have up to showcase pages.

To create one, click on the **'Me'** button, and under **'Manage'**, select your Company Page. Then, go to **'Admin Tools'** → **'Create a Showcase Page'**.

Have Your Employees Connected

Your biggest advocates on LinkedIn are your employees. Having them as followers means that you have access to their networks and connections, which can significantly expand your reach and bring more traffic to your Company Page. Encourage your employees to be linked with your Company Page to increase brand awareness.

Keep Followers Informed

The best way to boost your audience is to keep the one you have satisfied. Make sure to regularly publish valuable content such as articles, blog posts, or other updated on your company. Also, if you can think of an external article that can be valuable to your followers, do not hesitate to publish it as well.

Choose LinkedIn Groups

LinkedIn Groups offer a great way for you to connect with people from your field that are outside of your immediate circle. Being active in a LinkedIn Group and engaging in discussions can drive more traffic to your Page.

Want to find a Group that will match your goal? You can check out some LinkedIn suggestions with the **'Group Discover'** option, or simply use the search bar if you know what you are looking for.

Go Global

If you have customers in some countries where English is not the official language, then you might want to consider adding a description of your company written in other languages. Don't worry, you don't have to hire a translator for that purpose. LinkedIn offers multi-language tools that can take care of this for you.

Publish at the Right Times

Just like the strategies for your other platforms, your LinkedIn publishing must also be planned for. LinkedIn research says that the best time for content publishing on LinkedIn is in the morning and after business hours. This is when people are the most engaged, so you might want to take advantage of this information and schedule your post for then.

Advertising on LinkedIn

If you want to target your message to other professionals, whether CEOs or influencers, then advertising on LinkedIn is definitely something you should take advantage of. Once you determine *what* you want to advertise and *who* is your target audience, then you can proceed with the next steps.

Step #1: Your 'Campaign Manager' Account

First of all, to begin, you have to have a **'Campaign Manager'** account, which you can take care of here https://www.linkedin.com/ad-beta/login. This is a tool that helps you manage and optimize your ads in the most convenient way possible. Plus, this tool offers some beneficial tools that will display the performance of your ads, so that's an added bonus.

Step #2: Choose the Type of Your Ad

Next, you have to select the type of ad you want to promote. There are three options available:

192

1. Sponsored Content

2. Text Ads

3. Sponsored InMail

You can also create your campaign with all of the three formats to ensure the maximum possible reach.

Once you select the type of ad, enter the name of your campaign, choose the language of your target audience, and choose the call-to-action option, which is available only for the Sponsored-Content ads.

Step #3: Create the Ad

The best thing about the Campaign Manager is that it walks you through the steps of creation, offering you tips and help along the way. Follow the steps choosing the options that match your goal the most.

Step #4: Target the Ad

At this point, make sure that your ad will be targeted to the right people. You need to specify some criteria such as location, school names, company names, degree, job title, gender, age, years of experience, skills, etc. Make sure to save your criteria, so that you can speed things up the next time you wish to advertise on LinkedIn.

Step #5: Set the Budget and Schedule

There are three ways in which you can pay for the ads:

1. Cost Per Click (CPC)

2. Cost Per Impression (CPM) – for the messages in a member's view

3. Cost Per Send – for the Sponsored InMail ads (here, you pay only for those messages that are received)

For the CPM and CPS option, you are allowed to set a maximum daily budget you are willing to spend, and a bid price.

After that, simply schedule the start and end date and time for the ad, and you're done.

Is Your Marketing Strategy Working?

If you are pulling your metrics from another social media platform, then you are probably missing out on the real picture of your LinkedIn performance. The best way to check if your marketing strategy is working, is by checking out the built-in analytics tool on LinkedIn.

Go to the toolbar fount at the top of your page and click on the **'Analytics'** button. You will see that there are three available options:

Visitors - This is where data on the people who visit your page is stored. Here you can see the general overview of page view, the traffic metrics, you can isolate data from a specific time and date, see data from different pages on your profile, as well as see detailed information of the members who view your page (job function, location, industry, etc.)

Updates – Here you can find data about the content you share. These engagement metrics include the impressions, clicks, shares, likes, clicks, etc.

Followers – In the 'Followers' category, you can check out your list of followers in more detail.

Pinterest

Pinterest is that interesting platform where people plan their kids' unrealistic birthday parties. It is your go-to place when you are in need of inspiration, whether it is for remodeling your living room, getting a new haircut, or buying a pair of sneakers. But if you think that just because Pinterest is so much different than Facebook and Instagram, it is not worth the investment of time, money, and effort, for the purpose of promoting your brand, you cannot be more wrong.

It is the fact that people go there for inspiration that makes Pinterest a great platform for marketing your business. When your potential customers are searching for inspiration and solution, your products or services can be the thing that can solve their problems. And as Pinterest's motto suggests, this platform is perfect for reaching to your customers while they are making a decision.

Using Pinterest for Business

If you have a personal Pinterest account, you are probably familiar with their boards and pins. *Pins* are the images or videos that people save to their Pinterest account, while *boards* are the collections where pins are stores and organized (you'd want to keep the inspirations for your kid's birthday party in a different board than the one with your stew recipes).

But even though you may consider yourself to be a Pinterest guru, please, do not skip this chapter as business Pinterest is used differently.

Creating Your Business Pinterest Account

To market your business on Pinterest, you will need a business Pinterest account. This account is different as the one for personal use, as it offers the opportunity to advertise your content, as well as to track your metrics with Pinterest analytics.

To open a Pinterest business account, go to https://www.pinterest.com/business/create/, enter your email address and password, and click on **'Create Account'**. You will be asked to enter the name of your business, your website, as well as to choose the category that your business falls into.

Once you create your business account, you will see your feed page. This is only what you see. Your customers will only see your profile, which you can access by clicking on the red tack found in the upper right corner.

Completing Your Profile

Your profile may be created, but in order to be appealing to your followers, you will need to put in some work. First, you will need to have a profile picture uploaded. Click on **'Settings'** under your profile icon at the top right corner, scroll down, and upload your desired profile picture. Again, choose something that represents your business.

In the **'About'** section, make sure to add relevant information, use important keywords, and present your business in the best light possible. Add the location of your company and your website's URL. Once you're all set, click on **'Save Settings'**.

Confirming Your Website

This is probably the most important step when it comes to Pinterest marketing, as confirming your website throws a lot of benefits your way. Having a confirmed website will help you pinpoint what customers pin from your website, and will also add your logo next to each of the pins made from your website. And most importantly, having a confirmed website will increase you're the ranking of your Pins in search results.

To confirm your website, go to **'Settings'** and click on **'Confirm Website'** from the profile section.

Then, copy the text and paste it into the HTML of the index page of your website. Hit **'Finish'**.

Your Pinterest Boards

Now that your business account is ready, it is time for you to create your Pinterest boards so your customers will have a reason to follow you. Keep in mind that your customers don't need to follow your entire account. Once you create your boards, they can choose to follow one or multiple boards.

To start creating your boards, go to your Pinterest profile:

1. Click on the **'Boards'** tab, then hit the red '+' sign in order to create a new board.

2. Enter the desired name for the board. Make sure to use compelling and clear name for your board, and do not forget the keywords. Try to keep the name below 20 characters; otherwise it will get cut off in the search results.

3. To enter more details to your board, go back to the **'Boards'** tab, and click on the pencil icon.

4. Below the name, you will see that you need to enter a description. Describe what your board is about, keep in mind the keywords,

and try to be as to-the-point as possible. Then, choose the category of your board.

5. If you are ready to start pinning, you can go right ahead, but if you are still unsure, know that you have the option to keep the board secret until you are ready to make it visible. That way, you can save your pins but your followers will not see them until you turn off the **'Secret'** option.

The Pinning

After creating your boards, the next step is to add some pins to them. The most convenient way to do so is to have a Pinterest browser button installed, which you can find here https://about.pinterest.com/en/browser-button. With the help of that button, you can Pin things with a few clicks:

1. After installing your Pinterest browser button, click on the Pinterest icon from your toolbar.

2. There, you will see a list of available options, choose your preferred image, then click **'Save'**.

3. Add your description.

4. Select the board that you wish to save the Pin to.

If you're using the mobile Pinterest app, things will be even simpler.

To choose the cover pin for your board, go to the **'Boards'** tab, and click on the pencil icon. Click on **'Cover'** → **'Change'** and then select your desired Pin.

Your Pinterest Strategy

Just like with other social media platforms, you also need to have a few tricks up your sleeve when it comes to marketing your brand on Pinterest. Here are some simple tips that will make your Pins' ranking skyrocket and get you more followers.

Create a User-Generated Board

The best way about Pinterest marketing is that you can let your followers contribute to your boards by adding their own pins there. This is a great opportunity for you to get in touch with your audience as well as to keep them engaged and interested in your products or services. Select a few of your top followers and dedicate a Pinboard to them. Ask them to pin images that display what they like and appreciate the most about your products and services. For instance, if you are offering a huge sale, your customers may Pin images of a fancy dinner that they paid with the saved money from the discount. This is a very unique way to showcase customer testimonials.

Pin Consistently and at the Right Time

Pinning once a day is optimal for the promotion of your brand on Pinterest. Pinterest says that its peak times are the evenings and the weekends, so you might want to take advantage of that. Pin once a day, in the evening, and consider to pin twice on Saturday or Sunday, when people are most active.

But Pinterest says that the key does not lie in the number of times you pin per day, but in the consistency. For instance, if you have 12 images to be pinned this week, then it is recommended to pin twice a day (two days only once), rather than pinning once a day and leaving the remaining 7 pins for the weekend.

Focus on the Visuals

Pinterest is a visual platform, which means that creating images of high-quality is not an option, but a must. If you do not have the skill or the right to tools to create your own, you may want to consider hiring someone for the part, or even purchasing some stock images to pin.

Also, try to showcase your product or service the best way possible. For instance, instead of pinning a close-up of your sunglasses, why not upload an image of a model on the beach, wearing your sunglasses. Pinterest says that those Pins that display people using a product are 67% more likely to drive sales.

Go for Rich Pins

Rich Pins are those Pins that contain additional info (metadata pulled from your website) about what your followers will find when they click on your Pins. For instance, Rich Pins for recipes include the ingredient list and also the button **'Make It'**, which is a great call-to-action. These Pins are also great for articles, products, apps, and in other words, almost anything that Pinners are looking to find.

Advertising on Pinterest

Similarly to the previously-explained advertising campaigns, promoting your brand on Pinterest also require a step-by-step process to go through. Here is how you can easily create a Pinterest ad campaign:

Step #1: Install the Pinterest Tag

Pinterest Tag is a tool that shows you what actions people take on your website after your Pins redirect them there. This super-important tool will show you the sign-ups, checkouts, and searches that your followers make there, which will give you a clear insight of just how well your ads are performing. You can install the Pinterest tag here https://business.pinterest.com/en/pinterest-tag.

Step #2: Choose Your Objective

When you go to https://ads.pinterest.com/, the first think you will need to do is to select the objective from your ad. Here, there are only 4 available objectives:

1. Boost the Brand Awareness

2. Get Traffic to Your Site

3. Increase the Installs for Your App

4. Build an Awareness for Your Brand with Video Views

Step #3: Set the Budget

Here, you will be prompted to enter the name of your campaign, as well as to set the daily and lifetime budget.

Step #4: Create an Ad Group

Add groups are there to help you reach multiple goals for a limited budget, and within one ad campaign. It is recommended to launch 2-4 pins per an ad group.

Step #5: Choose the Target Audience

Go through the parameters for audience targeting and enter the desired preferences. Your target audience can be set based on the: gender, age, location, language, and devices.

Step #6: Choose the Ad Placement

At this point, you need to choose where your ad will be placed. If you have the means for it, choose the recommended, ALL placement. If not, you can either choose *Browse* (these placements end up in the user's home feed as related pins) or *Search* (these placements are recommended for keyword targeting).

Step #7: Add Keywords and Interests

To further optimize your targeting, you should take advantage of interests and keywords. This feature will ensure that your ads are targeted to the relevant searches. You have over 3400 interests to choose from, so you can rest assured that you will find the best ones for your business. For best results, use twenty-five keywords. You can also use negative keywords if there is something you want to exclude from the search.

Step #8: Set the Budget and Schedule

Enter the start and end date of your campaign and select how much you are willing to spend, on daily and lifetime basis. Make sure to make no mistake here as this option cannot be edited and changed later on.

Step #9: Optimization and Delivery

Here, set the maximum bid for your Pinterest ad. The minimum bid is $2.

Step #10: Determine the Pacing

You have Standard Pacing and Accelerated Pacing to choose from. The standard option is what aligns the bids and spending with the duration of the campaign, while the accelerated pacing enables fast delivery of the budget, and is recommended for those campaigns that have higher impact. To keep it simple, the standard pacing will not spend over your set limit, while the accelerated option can spend your limit way before the end date of your campaign.

Step #11: Select the Pins

Click on **'Pick a Pin'** to select the Pins you wish to add to your ad group. As mentioned earlier, each of your ad group should have between 2 to 4 Pins. In order for your Pins to be able to be added to your ad group they have to be saved on your profile and not on a secret board, have URLs (not shortened), and they shouldn't feature some third-party videos or GIFs.

Pinterest Analytics

Pinterest Analytics, unlike the Pinterest Tag, provides valuable information about which of your Pins perform best on the platform, not your website. This helpful tool offers metrics that allow you to keep a track of the performance of the Pins in order to gain insight of what should be changed and improved on your business Pinterest profile, in order to drive traffic and get more followers.

Besides the metrics, here you can also see the boards that people saved your Pins to, which can help you determine what people associate your business with and what they think about your brand and the products and services that you are offering.

To access your Pinterest Analytics, go to your profile and click on the **'Analytics'** tab found in the upper left corner.

The best metrics to track with Pinterest Analytics are:

Impressions – They measure the reach of your content and represent the number of Pins that appear in the search results, home feed, and category feeds.

Closeups – This represents the number of time that people tap on your Pin in order to have a better look at it.

Clicks – The number of re-directs from your Pins to your website.

Repins – This shows the number of time Pinterest users saved your Pin to their boards.

Top Pins – Here are displayed the pins that have been performing the best in the last month.

Top Boards – Your most popular boards in the last 30 days.

All-Time Stats – This is a long-view data great for determining what has worked for your Pinterest profile and what, in order to optimize your account.

Audience Affinities – Affinities show you the type of content that your audience is most engaged with.

Conclusion

Now that you've learned all about social media marketing, the next step is to create your accounts and get started with promoting your brand online.

But remember, this is not your magic bullet. A good marketing strategy can only be successful if you invest time, effort, and most importantly if you engage with your audience.

The social media marketing climate may seem unstable, but the forecast is definitely bright for brands who listen, learn, and want to improve and optimize for successful results.

Social Media Marketing
2019

The Must-Know Practical Tips and
Strategies for Growing Your
Brand, Becoming an Influencer
and Advertising Your Business
Using Facebook, YouTube, Twitter
and Instagram

By Gary Clyne

Table of Contents

Introduction

Did you manage to create your social media accounts but got stuck on your way to successfully promoting your brand? If your business is already present on social media but you struggle to grow your following and get your audience to engage with your content, you are at the right place.

You don't have to try too hard and overly promote yourself in order to draw customers. You just need to funnel your posts and take the right action that has helped many small businesses grow huge. This book is packed with tried-and-true methods of attracting potential customers with scroll-stopping content that will bring value to your fan base. So, if you are wondering why your Instagram posts don't have as many likes as your competitor's account or why your YouTube videos go unnoticed, the answers can be found in this guide.

Providing you with advanced marketing tips and techniques that will bring you the social media fame that your brand deserves, this book will show you that having thousands of followers doesn't necessarily mean having thousands of dollars to spend.

Ready for your visually stunning journey that will lead you to tons of new customers and a well-established brand? Join me on this knowledgeable social media ride and learn how to take advantage of the social media platforms to help your business grow.

Social Media Marketing – The New Era of Brand Promoting

What is the first thing that comes to your mind when someone mentions *marketing*? Newspaper ads? Radio pitches? Boring TV commercials? Direct mail? Or even manipulation? In the past, this was the only way in which businesses could reach customers. In the golden years of television, all you had to do in order to promote your brand to the world was to have a giant budget. Huge budget plus your product on TV equaled a guaranteed hit. But high budgets were for the really successful companies. And even though the invention of cable did bring some extra marketing opportunities, for small businesses, promoting their brand to customers was nothing but a pipe dream. Fortunately, the birth of the Internet shook things up and created new and much more affordable ways for marketing and communicating in general.

It is true that traditional forms of marketing still exist, but unlike before, having a Newspaper ad today is not a main marketing strategy, but an additional promoting technique to help businesses further expand their audience reach. Things have changed significantly, even up to a point where having a huge budget doesn't necessarily mean instant success. Nor does having a celebrity promoting your brand. The key to successful marketing is satisfying thek customer's needs.

Now, the modern consumer has increased needs and higher expectations than people did back in the TV's golden era. When purchasing a product or a service, people expect to get a personalized buyer's experience. And, instead of just watching a TV commercial and heading to the store, people now have much more exciting ways to explore their options and embark on their buying journey.

Today, a shopper may decide to visit your online store, do a price research on their smartphone, check the product's reviews online, watch a testimonial video, or even solicit feedback from friends on social media, all in order to determine whether purchasing your product will be worth it. So, it's easy to understand why funneling your budget only to customer acquisition no longer satisfies these complex buyer journeys. In order to build an engagement with their customers that will lead to positive customer experience and brand advocacy, businesses are now faced with reaching the customers across many different channels. Most of these channels are found on *Social Media*.

The moment that social media became a hit, businesses jumped on the bandwagon on promoting their services there. Why? Because social media is where most of your customers are. Marketing on social media is the quickest and most cost-effective way to reach your target audience.

But unlike traditional marketing that allowed very limited marketing opportunities for companies smaller than the large corporations, social media marketing is, in fact, more beneficial for small businesses. Marketing on social media is not a strategy about gaining millions of followers but about having customers that are engaged.

The new era of marketing has surely changed in favor of small businesses. Here is how they have more advantages on social media than the large companies with 6-figure budgets:

Individual-eFocused. One of the biggest differences between large- and small-scale companies, is that small businesses are actively involved in their communities and heavily focused on individuals. Customers have much more appreciation for smaller businesses as they tend to foster solid communication with individual customers. Take advantage of that!

Joint Marketing Efforts. When small businesses join forces, it can result in a very profitable outcome. And the social media platforms offer a great way for businesses to collaborate on their marketing strategies. Offering discounts, coupons, and demos are all great examples of this kind of strategies. For instance, you may partner up with another business and each of you to offer a discount of 30% for the other brand's products when a purchase of a particular product of yours is made. That way the customer pays less, both businesses profit, and everybody's happy. Obviously, this should be done with neighboring business only, not competitors.

Benefits from Big Advertising. You don't have to do the advertising yourself in order to profit. Some large corporations actually hold events that you can leverage in your own promoting techniques. For instance, American Express holds a Small Business Saturday, which is an event that encourages customers to shop small. By only posting that you will participate in such an event, you get to reap the benefits with almost no hassle involved.

Personalized Experience. Did you know that more than half of the consumers say that they are more likely to shop from smaller businesses because of the personalized attention they get? Since large corporations don't get the time to provide a personalized experience to each customer, this is something that small businesses can leverage in their social media marketing strategies. When customers come to your business, take the time to really connect. Genuine and timely responses and taking the time to understand what the customer is looking for in order to provide the best service for them, are both great examples of personalized attention.

As you can see, social media really did change the one-dimensional and boring traditional way of marketing for the better. However, keep in mind that all of those well-known, tried-and-true strategies still very much apply to marketing, even on social media. Social media marketing may be the new marketing era, but it is still the same world.

Your Best Strategy for Marketing on Social Media

Embarking the social media marketing train unprepared can be a deadly journey. Many businesses open their social accounts on an ad hoc basis; just because they think it is expected of them to be present there. However, not being present is sometimes better than being active without fully understanding what to do and how to be engaged. In order to be able to reap the benefits that social media marketing provides (web traffic, reaching customers, spreading brand awareness, building up loyalty, etc.), you need a well-planned marketing strategy that will help you stand out and slay the competition.

And while it is true that every social media platform requires a unique approach and differently-optimized technique, there are a set number of steps that businesses should take on each platform, in order to create their best marketing strategy:

227

Step #1: Set SMART Goals

Being on social media without knowing why exactly you have signed up in the first place is not how you should start your social media marketing. Having a set of goals that you wish to achieve is the best starting point for any marketing strategy. However, if your goals are set just for the sake of it, they may not help build up the most suitable strategy for you. To ensure that they are created with the purpose of finding the best marketing technique, your goals should fit into your plan as a whole, and most importantly, they should be set in a way in which you'd like your business to progress. For that purpose, -your goals should be SMART:

Specific – Specific and focused on identifying a concrete   outcome
Measurable – Defined success to evaluate progress and   strive   towards   its   achievement
Attainable – Challenging and yet reasonable to achieve

228

Relevant - Real and set to determine whether your efforts are worthwhile to you **T**ime-Bound - Realistic time frame for achieving your goal

Step #2: Understand Your Audience

Making assumptions can be dangerous. In order for you to provide value to your customers, you first need to know what it is that they are looking for. Keep in mind that every social media audience is different; you fan base on Instagram and your connections on LinkedIn want different things. Researching your audience prior to taking the plunge of promoting your brand is essential.

Luckily for you, there are many different tools that can help you take a glance at the newest social media demographic data to find the best approach for your social media platforms.

Step #3: Determine Your Metrics

Many businesses spend their time, money and effort promoting their brand, without stopping to take a look at how far they have gone. Regardless of the product or service you are trying to sell, the marketing strategy you take on social media should always be driven by data. The "likes" and number of followers you get are surely great to have, but if they do not turn out to be meaningful and result in customer engagement, they are really useless. Here are the metrics that matter the most when trying to understand whether your social media marketing strategy is successful:

Reach – The number of users that saw what you had shared. Check to see how far your reach actually spreads across the platform and whether it reaches the feeds of the audience.

Engagement – The number of interactions divided by the total number of impressions. This shows you what the audience thinks of you and whether they are willing to engage with your content.

Clicks – This represents the number of times people clicked on your content, logo, or the name of your company. When having a campaign running, these clicks are a great indicator of the things that encourage your audience to buy.

Organic and Paid Likes – These are the likes you get from paid or organic content, and they can be a great way to determine the type of content that attracts more audience and why.

Hashtag Performance – Everything related to hashtags can be found here. From the hashtags that are most associated with your business to the hashtag that brought the most engaged audience.

Sentiment – This measures the way in which your audience react to your content, hashtag, or overall brand. The sentiment digs a bit deeper and lets you know what people actually think about your brand and social media presence.

Step #4: Check Out the Competition

No matter what type of business you are trying to promote, chances are, the social media platforms are already packed with competition. Inspecting what your competition is offering to your target audience is a great way for you to determine what the weaknesses and strengths of the competitor brands are, in order to try and exploit them. Sneaky, right?

Go through their social media accounts and see what they are offering. What is their approach? What are they mostly focused on? What are the keywords that they rely on? Answering these questions will help you learn what is missing and how you can improve your strategy to offer your potential customers even better experience.

Step #5: Create Engaging Content

Social media is centered around content, so it's only understandable why posting suitable and engaging content of high-quality should be the heart of your social marketing strategy. But if you think that you can promote your brand in every single post and provide nothing but sales pitches to your followers in order to turn them into customers, you cannot be more wrong. 43% of social media users say that they will most likely unfollow businesses that try to hard to make a sell and are overly promotional of their brands. Instead, users want unique and genuine content that provides value.

Creating user-generated content for that purpose can be quite beneficial. By sharing popular hashtags, you will let your audience see a rawer side of you, without having to do any work, really.

When creating content, do not forget the magic of the visual. Our brain is wired to process images way faster than textual content, so even when you have a textual announcement to make, try to stick a cute photo alongside. Visual content gets shared 40% more than other content types, so create your content with that thought in mind.

Step #6: Post at the Right Times

In order for you to get the maximum engagement possible, you need to post your content at the times when your target audience is active the most. Of course, this depends on what your business is about

233

and who your target audience actually is. For instance, if you are in the healthcare industry, the best time to post on Twitter is on Wednesday between 11 and 1 a.m. But, if you are in the Consumer Goods industry, then you should post on Saturday at 1 p.m. There are many factors involved when deciding on the right posting times on the social media platforms – from your industry sector to the age group and location of your target audience - and the truth is, calculating on your own can be quite overwhelming. Instead of doing everything manually and by yourself, invest in a good tech tool that will not only do all the work for you, but will also show flawless and highly-accurate results.

Step #7: Engage

Social media is the place to connect with people and interact. If you want to stand out and be successful, you shouldn't just broadcast your content to your audience, but engage with them on a regular basis, as well. Create a custom hashtag to encourage discussions and get more engagement from your audience, but be prepared to respond to every social mention of your brand to show users that your customers are your number one priority.

Ideally, you should respond to all customers' requests and inquiries within 4 hours, as that is the wait time that most users expect. The average response time is 10 hours, so make sure to be one of the businesses who doesn't live their customers waiting for a response.

Step #8: Track and Improve

No matter how much you plan your strategies, things rarely go as expected. You will need to track your most relevant metrics in order to know just how your marketing strategy is progressing. That is the only way in which can learn what works and what should be improved in order to adapt your technique and bring more value to your customers for a successful promotion.

Prioritizing the Top Platform for Your Brand

One of the main reasons why people fail to establish a successful social media marketing is the fact that they prioritize the wrong social media platform. It doesn't matter if most of your friends are active on Facebook. That is not an indicator that you should bet your entire budget on Facebook advertising. Just because most of the people you know are addicted to a particular social media network doesn't mean that majority of your target audience have active accounts there.

Even though it is required that you have a strong presence on each of the most popular social media platforms, you need to pinpoint exactly which one of them you need to focus on the most. Otherwise, you might be spending your resources on an account that garners insufficient customer engagement. To provide value to your customers, you need to allocate your resources more efficiently. Having a hard time deciding which social media platform works best for your business? Read on to determine where you should be spending your budget the most.

Facebook

Facebook is the biggest social media platform and should be approached as such. Whether your audience is most active there or not, a Facebook presence is a definite must. But is the majority of your target audience really there?

Facebook is best for B2C businesses, and in some cases B2B as well. The top industries that thrive from Facebook marketing are:

- Fashion

- E-commerce

- Real Estate

- Health and Wellness

- Retail

- Sports

- Marketing

- Auto

- Entertainment

- News and Information

In 2018, the most common age demographic was from 25 to 34. The target age and gender are both men and women aged from 25 to 55+.

Did you know that Facebook is considered to be an SEO signal on a local level? That means that search engines check your Facebook profile in order to give relevant local search results.

Twitter

Twitter is also best for B2C businesses, although some B2Bs may also be at an advantage at this platform. The top industries that benefit from Twitter are:

- News and Information

- Travel and Hospitality

- Retail

- Health and Wellness

- Telecom

- Sports

- Finance

- E-commerce

- Sports

The most active audience on Twitter are both men and women from 18 to 29 years of age.

Twitter is the perfect spot for customer service. Whenever a customer comes across an issue with a product or service they cannot solve, they Tweet the business hoping to get the solution. Twitter has definitely become the central hub for customers, so make sure to take advantage of his platform and show off your expertise to the world.

Did you know that 93 percent of the people on Twitter who follow SMBs plan to actually buy products or services from the small and medium-sized businesses that they follow?

Instagram

Instagram is also best for B2C businesses and if you have got a visual product, then this is probably the best platform for marketing your brand. On the first glance, Instagram may seem like nothing more than an app for sharing photos, but this platform seriously packs a punch, especially with the younger audience, as 64 percent of the active Instagram profiles are aged from 18 to 29 years. Women are slightly more active on this platform than men, but keep in mind that that's shifting.

The industries that benefit the most from marketing on Instagram are:

- Fashion

- Travel and Hospitality

- Arts and Crafts

- Beauty

- Food and Beverage

- Photography

- Event Planning

- Health and Wellness

- E-commerce

- Auto

Did you know that 80% of all Instagram accounts follow a business? And what's even more interesting is the fact that 72% of them actually say that they have made a purchase of a product that they saw on Instagram.

Pinterest

Again, best for B2C businesses, Pinterest is a platform that every hobbyist is addicted to. Whether they are planning an event, remodeling their house, or saving yummy recipes, Pinterest is the paradise for everyone who is looking for inspiration and new ideas.

The most active group there are women between 18 and 45 years.

Pinterest is the perfect platform for these industries:

- Health and Wellness

- Retail

- Home and Garden

- Beauty

- Event Planning

- Fashion

- Food and Beverage

- Travel and Hospitality

- Arts and Crafts

- E-commerce

Did you know that whopping 87 percent of all active pinners have actually made purchases because of this platform?

LinkedIn

LinkedIn is a platform that is best for both B2B and B2C employment. If you are a business-to-business, then LinkedIn should definitely be the social media platform that you should prioritize.

The most active target group here are both men and women from 25 to 45 years of age.

The top industries that thrive the most on LinkedIn are:

- Financial

- Manufacturing

- Employment

- Legal

- Education

- Marketing

- Health and Wellness

- Science and Technology

- IT

- Professional Services

Did you know that the audience on LinkedIn actually has twice the purchasing power than the average audience on the web?

Another platform that you simply cannot afford not to be present on is **YouTube**. Although YouTube is surely different than the previously mentioned ones, it has proven to be of tremendous benefit for businesses of any kind. And while YouTube shouldn't be your main marketing platform, a strong presence there can be of extraordinary value for your business.

Marketing on Facebook

Facebook is, without a doubt, the most popular social media platform today. It is the place where people of all ages or backgrounds gather, in order to share details of their lives with close friends and family, as well as to stay in touch with people that they don't get to see often.

But the fact that this is what Facebook is mainly used for shouldn't discourage you. Quite the contrary. Having more than 2.3 billion of active monthly users gathered at one place is just what businesses need in order to raise awareness and grow a large customer community. Whether you are planning to use this platform for your main marketing strategy or not, it doesn't matter. Facebook is where most social media users are, and your place should definitely be among them.

Think Like a Follower

You cannot possibly expect for your marketing strategy to work if you fail to understand the reason why people may decide to follow you. Before you get all crazy with your posts and somehow expect an impossible level of engagement, it is important for you to know exactly what your fans are expecting from you.

Sure, the people who follow your brand on Facebook are definitely more likely to purchase a product or service from you. But keep in mind that they do not hit the 'like' button to buy from you. They are following your brand on Facebook because:

They Want a Discount – Most of your followers are expecting to receive some discounts at some points. Of course, this doesn't mean that you should give out coupons every day, but it will be beneficial if you make discounts a part of your marketing strategy.

They Want Updates and News – Fans follow brands also in order to stay updated with the latest products and services.

They Are Following Someone's Recommendation – A considerable amount of your followers will most likely hit 'follow' because a friend has recommended your brand and they are looking for the same positive experience.

They Are Looking for Like-Minded People – Many people follow businesses, news stations or shows, because they are looking for a way to talk about the things they are interested in with other enthusiasts.

They Want to Be Entertained – People want to be amused and entertained. You cannot possibly expect that your business-related stats will encourage your fans to engage. You need to provide them with engaging visual content in order for them to be interested in what you have to offer.

They Want to Express Loyalty – Most of the customers that enjoy your product/service online will most likely want to seek you online and become your follower. Believe it or not, many of your followers will be people just wanting to show support for the brand they believe in.

They Want to Ask a Question –With the rise of social media, who wants to dial customer service and spend their time waiting on hold? Most of the customers that want to ask your business a question will become your follower and do it online.

They Want to Give a Feedback - Many people will choose to become your follower in order to leave their honest feedback regarding your services or products.

Knowing what your followers are looking for and why they have decided to follow your brand the first place, is a great advantage that will be pretty helpful in strengthening the relationship with your customers.

Boosting Your Facebook Page

Assuming that you already have an up-and-running Facebook page, the next step is to give it a few boosts and start using it actively in order to reach to the people that matter the most to your brand.

Improving the Visibility

Optimizing your Facebook page in order to improve its visibility is (alongside creating quality content, obviously) the most important thing when it comes to marketing your brand on Facebook. Your business is competing with millions of other brands on this platform and, in order for you to stand out, you need to make sure that, when searching for something similar (whether on Facebook or in the Search Engines), people will come across your brand. Here are 4 incredibly important optimization tips that you cannot afford to miss out on:

#1: Combine the Name of Your Page with a Keyword

Choosing the right name for your page is of crucial importance for the visibility of your brand on Facebook. But, don't confuse this with your username. Your username is the identifier for your page on Facebook, and it is a unique name found at the end of your URL. It is showed in your page under the '@'symbol. This is not your page name. Your page name is the title of your Facebook Page that is shown in the search results.

If your business is unique and doesn't share common words with similar businesses or is already a well-established brand (think Quaker Oats or Ben & Jerry's), you can use nothing but your business name as a name for your Page. But, if your business is niched or has recently been founded, then you need to take a different approach. If that is the case, you might want to consider combining your business name with a keyword or a keyword phrase. Why? Because people who are looking to make a purchase online use keywords, not brand names.

For instance, if you own a pastry shop called Violet Delights you may find that there is already a 'Violet Delights' page on Facebook under the Fashion Designer and Boutique Store category. That means that using only your business name is probably not a good idea. Instead, combine it with some keywords to optimize your visibility. Naming your Page something like: Violet Delights London Pastry Shop, will make sure that your page shows up in related searches for pastry shops in your area.

#2: Customize Search Snippets

Your 'About' section is the place where you should let people know what your business is all about, where they can find you, how to get in touch with you, and things of that sort. But, what you probably didn't know is that the text you provide in this section can also be used for forming search snippets that will show up in the results on both Facebook and Google.

Try to share the information about your business in a way that can be easily converted to a search snippet. Try to add the most important info in a short and up-to-the-point format that people can see in their search results even before clicking on your Page in order to draw more attention to your Facebook Page.

#3: Complete the Info to Make Your Business Visible Locally

Remember how we said that Facebook is a local SEO signal? That means that when you go online to search for pastries shops, Google and Facebook consider your location first and display the pastries shops that can be found in your area.

This feature is especially beneficial for small, local businesses. In order to make sure that your Facebook Page will be shown on the local search results, you need to first complete all of the relevant info for your business such as: Country, City, Address, Zip Code, Phone Number, Working Hours, etc.

#4: Incorporate Keywords in the Content You Post

Keywords, keywords, keywords. Once you begin your social media marketing journey, keywords will be the term that you will constantly bump across. I, personally, cannot stress the importance of using relevant keywords enough. Why? Because it is impossible for you to gain organic or paid reach if you do not know what your potential customers are searching for in order to find the services that you provide. Once you know the keywords that are relevant for your business (you can use tools such as Google AdWords Keyword Planner), you should start incorporating them in your posts, the image and video descriptions, titles, etc.

However, using relevant keywords may also turn out to be not that productive if the competitions for those specific keywords is high. In that case, you will have to find other relevant phrases that are not used as often. https://moz.com/explorer is a great tool that can get the job done for you.

Enhancing the Timeline Tactically

Even though your Facebook page may be pretty much set up, without some tweaking it may look pretty bland. There are some finishing touches that you need to add in order for your page to be more appealing to your audience. Here are three simple things you can do to your timeline in order to enhance the look of your Facebook Page and create a stronger relationship with your audience:

Pin Content

Pinning Content is just what the name suggests. Pinning your most important posts and making them stick to the top of your timeline, which means that, even though you may continue posting, that post will still be top post your audience will see when they look at your Page. Your posts will stay *sticky*, until you decide to unpin them.

This is great for highlighting special product announcements, great discounts, promotional campaigns, or other limited offers. But what's even greater about this feature is that it gives you a perfect opportunity to welcome new followers and tell what your business is all about in a fun and engaging way. If you can, make a "welcome video" and pin it to the top with a short message like "Welcome to our page! If you are new here, take a

253

minute to watch our short but helpful video". Or, create a great welcome sign and pin the image to the top. The welcome message can be especially beneficial if you are just starting your Facebook journey.

Keep in mind that you can only pin one post at a time. Each pinned post will stay at the top for up to a week (of course, unless you decide to unpin it before that). To pin a post, just click on the pencil icon in the top right corner of your post. From the drop-down menu, select **'Pin to Top'**. To unpin the post, click on the pencil icon and select the unpin option.

Highlight a Post

Highlighting a post means expanding a certain status update across your Timeline, by taking up the space of both of the columns. Posts are highlighted with the purpose of drawing attention to some of your most important posts.

The fact that you can have many highlighted posts on your timeline makes a great highlighting strategy that can help you draw more traffic. Highlighted posts are great for grabbing the follower's attention when you are trying to introduce a new program or a service. You can create a series of images and have them roll out over a set period of time.

Another great strategy would be to highlight every customer testimonial. Whenever you see a customer share positive feedback about your product or services, turn that into a post, add an image of that customer, and highlight that post to make it really stand out.

To highlight a post, click on the star icon found in the top right corner of a post. To undo the highlighting, just unclick the star icon and the post will be no longer highlighted.

Keep in mind: Pinned posts will most likely make your posts more visible as they appear at the top of your timeline. Highlighted posts do not stay at the top, but are highlighted chronologically, and are pushed down across the Timeline with each new post that appears. The advantage of the highlighted posts, however, is that they have no time limitations. Also, have in mind that you cannot choose both pinning and highlighting for the same post. For each post, you are allowed only one option.

Create Milestones

Milestones are the perfect way for you to share the story of your business to your audience, through the power of images and words. The milestones are uploaded in chronological order and can appear anywhere on the Timeline, depending on the time and take you set. For instance, you can create a milestone for the day that your business was founded, even if that happened a hundred years ago. Obviously, this will be the oldest milestone.

To create a milestone, select '**Event, Milestones +**' from the drop-down menu in the status update bar.

By default, each milestone will be highlighted and then stretched across your Timeline.

Milestones are a great way for businesses to tell a story, but most brands fail to understand that the milestones can also be a part of their marketing strategy. Keep in mind that the more meaning you assign to the milestones, the more traction you will be able to see:

Include an Image – Do not just say that your business was founded in 1965. Include an engaging image that will capture the attention of your followers. If you need to, scan some old newspapers or photos to give your audience a more transparent look into the history of your business.

Include a Call-to-Action – Make sure to encourage your customers to find out more. Include a call-to-action by pasting a link that leads to more info about the created milestone. By doing so, you encourage people to take an action and potentially purchase a product or service.

By turning pins, highlights, and milestones into a strategy, you are more likely to use these amazing features on a regular basis, which can not only visually transform your Facebook Page and bring you more followers, but it will also encourage the audience you have to become more engaged with your content.

Take Advantage of Apps

To make your Page even more appealing to the eye, take advantage of different apps that allow you to share slides, poll your community, and approach your marketing strategy form an even more interactive angle. However, make sure not to get too crazy with all the bells and whistles. Those apps may turn out to put your followers off if they are used poorly. Be moderate with these extras and try not to go overboard.

Your Strategy for Encouraging Engagement

Facebook pages have become even more powerful than TV. Large businesses (think Coca Cola) can reach more people with a simple post update than with a TV commercial. And the best part? Facebook posts are free (unless you are paying for the advertisement, of course, in which case it is still a lot cheaper).

The content you post on Facebook should:

- Create brand awareness

- Establish expertise

- Drive traffic

- Have multiple goals

- Increase your community

- Drive sales without being a sales pitch

- Be proofread and well-constructed

- Be visually engaging

- Be on topic

259

- Be light and upbeat

However, once you start sharing your content with your audience, you will see that posting is easy. The part that is tricky, is having your followers engage with your content. In order for your audience to respond, they need to be compelled to do so. Attracting engagement may seem like a hard task, but with a few techniques under your belt, you can easily form a strong interactive relationship with your audience.

Structure Well to Get Answers

Sometimes, the best strategy lies in the way you create your content. Your posts should carry open questions that will attract your audience to comment and share their opinion. Your questions should be:

- Open – They should carry a discussion that is open-ended

- Easy – They shouldn't require too much thinking in order to attract a larger group. The answers should be given rather impulsively

- Timely – To get higher engagement, tend to ask questions that follow a hot topic or trend

Your questions should never be:

- Political – You shouldn't take a side as a brand, but if you are discussing a political issue without taking one, you will most likely be accused of not taking one. The secret formula is to steer clear from discussing politics

- Complicated – Philosophical questions are not for your brand's business page. The questions that require research are usually not answered on Facebook.

- Loaded – If your questions are pretty much self-explanatory and don't really require an answer, no one will bother to comment on them

Make Them Ask Questions

The tried-and-true way to make your audience interested in engaging with your brand is to give them the power to feel in charge. And the best way to do so is to provide your followers with the opportunity to ask you questions.

This will work the best if you create a topic or a theme for the questions, set an end date, and explain when and who will answer the questions. Just sure to put the right person for the job under the spotlight here in order to give the right answers.

You can present the answers in a video, a document, or even stream a Facebook Live streaming where the questions will be answered live, to further increase the engagement.

Use the Emojis

The best way in which you can illustrate sentiment is by using emojis in your posts. The use of emojis will not only make your content more attractive, but it will also give your audience the impression that your business is friendly. Those posts that include emojis have higher chances for like, comment, and share.

Ask for Feedback

You may think that asking your audience for feedback may seem as begging, but the truth is, people like to be included. By asking your followers to share their feedback on a certain product or service, you let them know that you value their opinion, and that is something that can do wonders for the level of engagement on your Page.

Generate Messenger Connections with a Discount in Your Post

The bots in Facebook Messenger are increasingly gaining in popularity. There are many tools for small businesses that provide you with the opportunity to automatically respond to a comment with a bot (https://manychat.com/ is a great tool for this purpose). But besides being used to enhance the shopping experience or give updates, you can take advantage of this AI communication by giving away discount. What am I talking about? For instance, a great tactic for increasing the engagement is asking people to comment on a post and giving them a coupon or discount in return. That way, many people will take the bait and engage with your content. Once the comment is shared, messenger bots will automatically reward them with the voucher.

Who doesn't like free stuff? Offers like this will encourage most of your followers to comment, but what's even more important for your marketing, is the fact that the traffic will send a signal to Facebook's algorithm that quality content is shared, which will only increase the visibility of your post.

Give Your Fans a Shout-Out

Spotted a follower wearing your company's t-shirt or drinking your coffee? Share the picture posted by your followers to show your audience how much you appreciate their positive feedback. But, before you hit the 'share' button, make sure to ask for permission from the original poster, and obviously, thank the contributor.

By thanking your audience for your loyalty, you will create a goodwill feeling that will most likely result not only in the engagement on that particular post but on your other content as well.

Create Facebook Events

Facebook events are the best way to show your audience that you are constantly working on something to provide them with more value. Creating Facebook events will not only let your followers know that you want to keep your community tight but also will allow you to gauge the interest of your audience.

Facebook events can include:

- Sale

- Tweet-Up (a meet-up on Twitter) or a Twitter Chat

- Party

- Conference

- Contest

- Webinar

The best thing about events is the fact that they are easy to set u, and you get to invite everyone that follows your brand on Facebook:

1. Click on **'Events'** found in the left menu of your home page.

2. Select + **Create Event.**

3. At this point, you can either choose to **Create a Public Event** if you want your event to be seen by everyone, even those that are not your followers, or **Create a**

Private Event, if you want only the people you invite to be able to see the event. Note that whatever option you choose, you will not be able to change it later.

4. Fill in the details such as the name of the event, the time and date, as well as write a compelling description.

5. Click on **'Create'**. You will then be redirected to a page where you should invite the people you want to invite to the even.

One of the biggest Facebook marketing mistakes that small businesses make is using Facebook Events to spam. If you invite people to events every other day, you will not only lose your brand's credibility and your existing audience, but you are also at risk of having your Facebook account suspended or shut down.

Give Facebook Groups a Try

Besides having a Facebook Page – which is absolutely necessary in order to market your brand on Facebook – as a business, you should also think about trying Facebook Groups as well. Facebook groups are different than Pages in a way that they allow only 5,000 people (Pages can have millions of followers), and that the conversation in Facebook Groups is a bit more expansive. Facebook Groups have dozens of conversations going a on daily basis and are the perfect opportunity for you to position your brand and find new customers.

With Facebook Groups you have two options:

1. You can join an existing Facebook Group with your personal profile

2. You can create your own Facebook Group

Joining a Facebook Group

If you think about skipping this option as you don't see how your business can benefit from this, you cannot be more wrong. Joining an existing Facebook Group that is managed by someone else, gives you the perfect chance for you to create awareness for your brand by being helpful. People tend to ask a lot of questions in groups. Find the ones where you can share your skills and expertise in order to resolve someone's issue, become a member and spread brand awareness. You can do this by giving outright answers, sharing a video, links to blog posts, or even mentioning your own services. This will not only let people know about your brand, but it will also reward you with extra followers.

Here is how you can become a member of groups and engage with people who you believe might be potential customers:

1. Log into your personal Facebook Profile.

2. Click on the **'Groups'** tab found in the left 'Explore' section of your Home page.

3. Once you are automatically sent to the **'Discover Groups'** page, you will see suggested groups by Facebook, based on the groups you've already liked or those that your friends participate in.

4. Once you find a group you wish to join, click the **'Join Button'**.

Keep in mind that Groups and Pages are different. Unlike simply clicking the 'Like' button and becoming a fan of a Page, you will have to be accepted in order to become a member of a group (unless it is Public). Also, some groups will ask you to give your answer to a few questions before you send your request. Once your request has been approved, a notification will be sent to you. You can then start a conversation or join existing ones.

Creating Your Own Facebook Group

As much as it is beneficial to be a member of a group that is managed by someone else, keep in mind that you have to play by others' rules. Deciding to create your own Facebook Group means you get to control the entire group, as well as gives you the opportunity to see the group as you see fit and for the purpose that helps your brand the most.

But, before you begin building your group, you will first need to decide what kind of the group you wish to create. There are three different ways in which most businesses use groups:

To Create a Community Around Products

Most of the business groups are created with the purpose of giving the customers a bonus for purchasing a particular product or service. By creating such a group where your paid customers will be members of, you reward them by making them feel privileged and exclusive. You can use these groups to give them additional tips or training for the products or services purchased.

To Establish Authority

You can also have a special group created especially for your email subscribers where you can share articles, tips, and tutorials on how to use your product or services.

To Build a Community Around a Specific Topic

You don't have to use your company's name for the name of your group. Instead, your group can be created to reflect a certain topic that your business has expertise in. For instance, if you are selling spices, one idea for your business is to create a group called "Spicy Homemade Recipes" and use your spices as ingredients for creating the delicacies. That way your customers will be given plenty of inspiration on how to use your products, and other people who are fans of spicy cuisine can also be drawn to your Group and Page and will most likely become potential customers.

Now that you know why you will use your Group, let's see how you can successfully create one.

Creating the Group

Log into your personal Facebook profile, and click on the **'Group'** button found in the left sidebar. Next, select the green **'Create Group'** option. A '**Create New Group**' dialogue box will appear, and you will be prompted to name your group, add some people, and select the privacy settings. *Important: You have to have at least one person to add to the group in order to create it!*

271

Depending on the goal of your business, your group can be:

Public – In Public Facebook Groups, the content is visible to anyone who decides to check the group out. Anyone can join a public Group and anyone can see the posts there. If your goal is to build a community around a specific topic, then a Public Group is perhaps the best choice.

Closed – Unlike with Public Groups, if someone wants to join a Closed Facebook Group, their request must be accepted by the Group administrator first. Here, the content can be seen only by the members of the Closed Group. Closed Group is the most popular type of Facebook Groups for businesses, as it creates a perfect opportunity for you to be picky about the people you let in, and ensures that no one other than the selected audience can get educated with your tips and tutorials for free.

Secret – In Secret Facebook Groups, it is not only the content that is secret, but the Group itself. Only the members can see the posts and the Group isn't listed in search results. The Secret Facebook Groups are best for businesses who are looking for a way to establish the authority of their business. These groups are created only for specific members and are a great way for your business to provide coaching. If you want to, you can even have your members pay a monthly fee to be a part of your Group.

Now that you have chosen the privacy level of your Group, click on **'Create'**. Your Group is now ready. All you need to do now is to load images and take care of the setting preferences and images.

Customizing the Group

Once your Group is all set up, the first thing you need to do is add a cover image. The recommended size is 828 x 315 pixels. Once the image appears, click on it, and add a description and the rules for the group.

Then, click on '**...**' in order to select the type of your Group. This obviously depends on your purpose. Would you like to educate, provide your audience with customer support, or create your group around a specific business' event? You can pick from Buy and Sell, Events and Plans, Family, Custom, Travel, Project, Support, Neighbors, etc.

Once you choose the type, the next step is to add your location, tags, web address and other contact info.

Now that your Group is ready to go, start posting. It is recommended to write down a post with the rules of your Group and pin it to the top.

Invite People to Join

The first mistake that most small businesses make, is the fact that they usually invite their friends and family to join first. As beneficial as they are to increase the number of followers on your Facebook Page, for your Group, your personal contacts may not be the best fit. Why? Because they usually are not paying customers. Your goal here should be to focus on the people that your Group will serve. Here are some tips that can help you find encourage the right people to join:

- Send an email to your subscribers introducing your Group and encouraging them to join

- Share the Group on your other social media platforms

- Invite the visitors of your website to join your Facebook Group

- Add a button on your website that will lead your visitors to your Group

- On your lead magnet's thank-you page, add an invitation for your visitors to join

Curate Content

Before you can find content to share on your Group, you will first have to determine what type should the content be. What will your strategy be? To sell?

275

To create a support group? To entertain? Once you make sure you are clear on that, you can find relevant content that is trending to share with your members.

Google News – If you want to share the most recent news article, there isn't the best place to look at, really.

https://buzzsumo.com/ - This gem will show you what the hottest topics are at the moment. Also, you can refine your search by searching for specific topics that are relevant for your group.

The most important thing is to stay as updated as possible and share topics that your Group members will be interested in interacting with.

Encourage Engagement

No strategy will be successful unless it yields in audience engagement. To make sure that your content will spark interaction, take advantage of some of these tips:

Tutorials – Make sure to post at least one tutorial video per week to keep your members updated with the latest product/service developments.

Polls – Struggling to find a new idea? Ask your members. Polls are a great way to check the audience's opinion as well as to get inspired.

Challenges – Challenges are perhaps the most attractive interactions among group members. Design a challenge of some sort and ask your members to join. You can even invite your members to work with you on a challenge, which is especially beneficial if your business provides services.

Live Q&As – A once-a-week live session for asking and answering questions is a great way to keep your Group members involved.

Daily Theme Prompts – Prompts allow people to post about a specific theme every day. Ask your members to post photos of your product/service. This will not only give them an opportunity to share something about themselves, but will also further expand the awareness for your brand.

Tip: As your Group grows, you may not be able to monitor and post actively. For that purpose, you should consider hiring a community manager to take care of that. Most groups' managers are the most active members of the groups. Look inside and find the ideal candidate.

Taking Advantage of Facebook Live

Think Facebook Live is just another social media vanity project? Well, think again because Facebook Live is just the thing your business needs in order to interact with customers in a more humane way. Unlike your regular video posts where you can just sit and hope that someone will comment, Facebook Live is not a one-way thing. Here, your audience is engaged to interact. In fact, it is the engagement that they find so appealing that makes Facebook Live so popular.

Broadcasting Live

There are two ways in which you can broadcast Live on Facebook. Through your Facebook profile and with the help of the Mentions app.

To stream Live <u>from your profile</u>, tap the 'Publish' option from your Facebook Page, and click on the **'Live'** icon. Once that option is chosen, in your status update bar, write down the description for the broadcast. This is the title of the Facebook Live and it is what will go out in the notifications and in the feed.

You will also have the option to choose the audience that you will broadcast to. You can either make it public, select only a group of people, or choose to be viewed by everyone who follows you. Then, click on **'Go Live'**. This is when the streaming will begin.

During your streaming, you will see the number of people who are viewing live, as well as the live comments that people are sending. This makes a perfect option for Q&As because you get to answer their questions in real time, which is what most customers appreciate the most.

After your broadcast is over, it will be saved on your Timeline just like any other video post.

To broadcast Live <u>through the Mentions app</u>. The process is pretty straightforward. Just, open the app, click on **'Post'**, and then select the **'Live Video'** option. The only difference here is that, unlike with your Facebook Page, the app doesn't give you the option to select your audience, as everything becomes public on your Page.

Improving Your Streaming

As beneficial as it is, if not done properly, Facebook Live can only make your business look unprofessional if caught unaware or unprepared. Here are some tips for you to improve your broadcast and provide high-quality streaming to your audience:

Have a Focus – The last thing you need is to be rambling in front of your audience live. For that purpose, be prepared in advance and have an outline of the things that you wish to talk about. Staying focused on the reason why you are streaming in the first place will help your broadcast seem natural and attract followers to engage.

Have a Compelling Title – Keep in mind that when people get notified that your business is about to go live, they only get the title of your broadcast. So, create your title with that in mind. Make sure it is a real attention-grabber that will encourage people to watch.

Use Both Cameras – If you are streaming from your Smartphone, make sure to use both the front and back cameras. No one wants to see you the camera move all the time, by toggling back and forth between the cameras on your phone, you will provide a much better video, even if one camera is of lower capacity.

Have a Great Audio – You can choose to speak clearly and loudly and that would be fine. However, it is recommended that you use a high-quality microphone for this purpose in order to provide a video of an even higher quality. Whatever you decide, the most important thing is to avoid broadcasting from a place where there are a lot of busy background noises.

Include a CTA – Ending your broadcast with a call-to-action is the most tactical way to finish your stream, as that way you direct your audience to a specific place. Whether it is to visit your website or share their thoughts on another post, the point is for the engagement not to end with the stream but to keep the audience as interactive as possible.

Edit the Videos

Once the streaming is over and the video is posted on your Timeline, you can choose to edit it just as you would edit any other video post. To do so, click on the date near the post and then select the **'Edit'** option.

Choose the Right Thumbnail – Facebook will give you ten different image options to be the thumbnail for your video, but you can also choose to upload your own, custom-made one. Unless Facebook's images are excellent, the latter option is recommended.

Choose the Category – Click on the **'Video Category'** and choose the right category for your video from the drop-down menu.

Include a Call-to-Action – Shop Now, Sign Up, and Learn More, are just some of the options that Facebook gives you to include as CTAs to encourage your customers to further engage. Since you've probably included a CTA in the video itself, make sure that this call-to-action matches the one from the streaming.

Increase the Reach – To further amplify your reach and become more visible, you may want to think about creating a video ad from your broadcast, through the Ads Manager.

Reusing the Stream

Just like with your other content, your Facebook Live broadcast should be used in as many different places as possible. The best way to do so is to write a blog post covering the most important things discussed in the broadcast. After having a good piece of content written, think about embedding the Facebook Live post or just adding the video.

You can then share the blog post across your other social media platforms to boost the audience engagement there.

I personally recommend embedding the Facebook Live post because that will get you more views on the video which will show on your Facebook page, which may result in even more followers.

Marketing on YouTube

You may think that your sheer presence on social media and the fact that you are posting regular content on YouTube are enough for you to gain thousands of views and a crowd that is willing to comment and engage with your videos, but once you begin marketing your brand on YouTube, you will soon realize that marketing success on YouTube goes beyond posting explainer and testimonial videos.

In order for your channel to attract many followers that plan on engaging with your videos, you will have to approach marketing more strategically. This chapter will give you some advanced tips on how to enhance your YouTube marketing journey.

Growing Your YouTube Channel

Your YouTube content should be optimized at every stage in order for it to compel users to watch, and more importantly, further engage with your videos. Having the next tactics up your sleeve may be just what you need to give your channel a boost and grow your following:

Make the Video Production Process Sustainable

Although this one goes without saying, the production's workflow is often the least tackled process in the making of videos. You may have a Hollywood-like budget to spend on your videos, but if it takes you too long to produce, your expensive videos are not going to grow your channel.

Regardless of the type of business you are trying to promote and the kind of video you want to film, you should know exactly what you want to achieve with your content and strive to develop and post it on a regular basis.

If you are serious about your YouTube marketing, then you might want to invest in a tiny video studio. It doesn't have to be anything fancy. A quiet place with a nice background, a camera that is ready to roll, and a microphone of high quality are enough for you to be ready to shoot at all times.

Hook Them Up from the Start

People start watching a video from the beginning, and if the beginning fails to sweep them off their feet, they will likely just go back to their silly cat videos instead. Strive to begin your videos with a great hook. For instance, if you are filming a project, make sure to show the end result first. For instance, if your video is for a cake recipe, show the baked and decorated cake first, to give the audience a taste of what they should expect to get by watching the whole thing.

Keep Your Opening Credits Short

Don't make your audience lose interest because of your long opening credit. Keeping mind that your followers have short attention spans, so make sure to have theirs hooked. Also, because long opening credit sequences are boring, people will be discouraged from clicking on another video of yours just to avoid watching the long opening again.

Instead, keep your opening short. Make it upbeat, punchy, and most importantly, not longer than 5 seconds.

Cut the Distractions Out of Your Videos

No matter howl prepared you are, chances are, when filming your videos, your mind will block at some point. Long pauses or bouncing from subject to subject can cause your audience to shift their view to the other videos in the recommendation sidebar instead. In order to keep them interested in what you have to say, you need to be interesting.

Once your video is filmed, watch it carefully and really pay attention to the details. Is it engaging enough to keep your audience compelled? If you veer from the subject too much, refilm it. If not, enhance it with some video editors that will allow you to smoothly cut from one shot to another. https://www.openshot.org is a great free tool that can help you edit your videos. The whole point is to make sure you are engaging and give your audience a reason to click away.

Improve Your Watch Time with Longer Videos

This may contradict the previous "keep your openings short" statement, given the fact that people have short attention spans, however, if your videos are to-the-point and engaging, longer duration can actually lead to more watch time, which will, in turn, enhance your content in the YouTube's algorithm.

Of course, the video should be longer if it makes sense to talk for minutes on that specific topic. The point still remains that you shouldn't come as boring or cause your followers to click away. The rule of a thumb is that videos between 7 and 15 minutes in length perform the best.

Use Older Successfully-Proven Tactics

Each of your videos will perform differently, and the truth is, you cannot possibly make them all to be successful. However, you can use the same tactics in order to strive to recreate the thing that makes your audience watch your top videos.

Dive into YouTube Analytics and see which videos perform the best. Then, spend some time watching and comparing, and try to find patterns among them. Is the subject similar? Are they edited with the same style? Is your mood brighter? Take notes of the similarities and try to incorporate them in future videos to boost up your ranking.

Your highest-converting videos can be found in the Creator Studio. Simply, go to **'Analytics'**→ **'Subscribers'** and then select **'YouTube Watch Page'**.

Develop Series

There is nothing that can improve your watch time like having videos that people will want to binge watch. Series playlists are the best way for you to create a great binge-watching experience for your audience, but in order to create them, you need to have uploaded videos as a series.

Your series can be developed based on the type of videos that has performed well, however, it is best to have more than one series, each of them covering a specific topic. For instance, if you have testimonial and explainer videos, create two series for each of the two topics, but also, use a different style for the thumbnails as well. That way your viewers can easily know what the video is about just by taking a quick look at the thumbnail image.

Using videos as a series means that if a viewer clicks on the video, YouTube will automatically have your next video to be Up Next at the top of the list of recommendations. The next video will automatically play after the current one is over, unless the viewer has turned off their AutoPlay option.

In order for you to turn a playlist into a series playlist, open **'Video Manager'**. Go to **'Playlists'** and click on the edit button found on the right of the playlist that you wish to change. Finally, click on **'Playlist Settings'** → **'Set as Official Series for This Playlist'**.

Go with the 'Hub, Hero, Help' Strategy

Using three different types of videos in your content strategy can be of significant importance for your YouTube channel. By choosing the 'Hub, Hero, Help' strategy, your videos have three different goals:

1. To serve the community of the channel
2. To be shareable
3. To perform well in search

Hub Videos are focused on the community and are created with the purpose to strengthen the bond between you and your viewers, as well as with your viewers with each other. In these videos, you should respond to comments, post live, or even share personal stories.

Hero Videos are videos that are specifically designed to yield success. They are mostly focused

292

on a hot subject, such as a news event or an upcoming holiday. Those videos are designed to encourage people to share them.

Help Videos to provide content that is easy-to-search and provides value that is actionable. Troubleshooting videos, DIY projects, and general how-to videos all fall under this category. If you want to find topics that people search the most at the moment, check out Google Trends and get the inspiration for your latest Help Video.

Adding these three types of videos to your content calendar can be quite beneficial, but only if you post them at different intervals. For instance, the best strategy is to upload one Hub Video each month, to post Hero Videos every 3 months, and to upload Help Videos on a weekly basis.

Team Up with Other YouTubers

You cannot do everything alone, and neither can the rest of the small businesses promoting their brands on YouTube. Collaborating with other

YouTubers and filming videos together is the best tactic to expose yourself to people who'd never have heard of your brand.

When two content creators collaborate with each other, that creates an endorsement. The video alone may be a good enough reason for the other brand's viewers to check your channel out, and click the 'Subscribe' button. Some of the hugest YouTube creators cross-promote their content, so why shouldn't you?

First things first, you need to find the perfect collaborator. Ideally, the other YouTuber should have a slightly large channel than yours, but don't obsess with the channel's size too much. The important thing is for the collaborator to offer a different content to a similar audience. For instance, if you are selling spices, you might want to consider teaming up with a local farmer and create recipes promoting their fresh ingredients and your unique spices.

There are tools who can help you find the right collaborator. https://socialblade.com/ offers a great way for you to compare metrics and find the perfect match. When selecting the right candidate, look at their location, gender, interest, age, and engagement.

Ultimately, you might just ask your audience for the collaborator. Ask them who they also like watching, or you can do the work yourself. Check out the channels of your audiences and look for the connection.

Improving the Performance of Your Videos

If you have some videos that sit forgotten on your Channel or are looking for a way to bring more exposure to the ones that are performing with mediocre success, there are some ultimate strategies that can help you boost the way your videos perform on YouTube.

Here are the 4 secrets for enhanced YouTube performance:

#1: Monitoring Your Target Audience

The biggest reason why your videos do not result in success is perhaps the fact that you are not providing solutions to the issues that your audience have. The first thing you need to do is to monitor the concerns that your audience has in order to make sure that your videos actually address these topics. There are some incredible tools that are specially designed for the audience listening, in order to improve customer experience. Some of the best tools for that purpose arehttps://sproutsocial.com/ and https://hootsuite.com/.

#2: Have Your Signature Production Style Ready

Having the right content created to address your audience issues is probably the most important step, however, it will not bring you any success if you fail to deliver the content the right way. Your videos need to be compelling, engaging, and most importantly, of high-quality. You don't necessarily have to go all crazy with expensive, professional equipment, but a shaky camera may sentence your video to a lifetime of loneliness on YouTube. Here are the most important things you need to consider when making the video:

- Have an eye-catching title

- Craft an engaging narrative

- Edit your video for success

- Focus on delivering value to your customers

- End with a call-to-action

#3: Increase the Discoverability with Creator Studio

Your video may be slow in performance due to the fact that they (as well as your channel) are not optimized properly. How can you possibly expect thousands of likes if your audience cannot find your videos in the search results easily? In order to improve your video's performance, increasing their visibility is a hugely important step.

Within your Creator Studio, you will find many optimization options that you need to take care of, such as: adding a custom thumbnail, optimizing your title with relevant keywords, including brief summaries of the videos (again with relevant keywords), provide URLs that will lead your customers to your website or other social media platforms, adding tags to help people find your video better, adding a comprehensive transcript, etc.

All of these will help you make your video more discoverable. Just make sure to hit **'Save Changes'** when you're done, and your audience will be provided with the chance to discover your videos easily.

#4: Promote Your Channel on Social Media

This is a no-brainer, really. The more you promote your channel on other social media platforms, as well as your blog, the more people will discover your YouTube videos. It's as simple as that, and yet, most businesses fail to do this the right way.

While simply posting URLs that lead to your YouTube channel on Facebook will bring some exposure, that doesn't necessarily mean that you will get more views and improve the overall performance of your videos. In order to boost how your videos perform, you need to promote them where the audience will have the best chance of seeing them.
By default, this should mean promoting on the

social media platform that your business prioritizes, however, there is more to it.

The best tactic is to check Google Analytics, not only to see which platform your audience uses the most, but to also do a split testing in order to determine which type of messaging they prefer. This will help you promote the right kind of videos to the right people in the way that they will appreciate the most.

When trying to improve the performance of your videos, keep in mind that the most important metric is the time watched, not the number of views. The more customers watch your video through to the end, the higher your rank on YouTube. These performance tips will help you improve your watch time, so make sure that each of your videos, as well as your channel is successfully optimized.

Generating Leads with YouTube

YouTube has an enormous lead potential, and yet, only a tiny portion of the small businesses actually have a channel there. That should encourage you to get more creative and start generating leads, before the rest of your competition realizes what they are missing out on and decides to tap into the golden potential.

Here are three tactics that will help you generate more views for your videos, drive traffic from your website, and increase the number of subscribers for your channel.

Driving Traffic with YouTube Cards

YouTube cards are the perfect trick up the marketer's sleeve, as they allow even further engagement on the uploaded videos. By adding a simple card on your video, you add a call-to-action to your content which will most likely provide you with additional interactivity. The links will direct the viewers where you want them to go and push them to take action and further engage.

Since this option was mainly created for the mobile users, it works seamlessly on all devices. That being said, you get the opportunity to send even those people that are watching your video via their mobile app, to your website.

How do YouTube cards work? When you add your card to your video, there will be a teaser window in the top right corner of your video. The teaser will be active for 5 seconds, meaning that the viewer has only 5 seconds to click on it, for the card to be revealed. If the viewer does not click on the teaser, in place of the card, the 'i' sign will appear.

You can easily add YouTube cards. The only thing you need to do is go to your **'Video Manager'** and find which video you want to add the card to. Open the drop-down menu found next to 'Edit' that is below your video, and click on **'Cards'**. Then go to **'Add Card'** and choose the type of card you wish to add (a link, video, channel, poll, or playlist) and click on **'Create'**. After selecting, you get to customize the card by, for instance, adding the URL for your Link card. Once you're all set, click on **'Create Card'.**

Now, all you have to do is to decide the spot where you want your card to be shown on your video. You can just drag the marker below the video to the spot where you want your card to appear.

Keep in mind that you will have the option to use additional cards, as well. However, if thinking about this option, you need to consider these:

- Your cards must be spaced out, so your viewers don't get too distracted. Otherwise, they might just click on something else from the recommendation sidebar.

- Even though adding multiple card may seem like a great way to encourage engagement, too many cards will most likely putt viewers off. Never use more than 3 cards for a higher rate of click-through.

- Do not use arrows that point to your cards. Not all devices show the videos the same way, and you might end up with an arrow that points in a totally different spot on the video, which let's face it, will look super spammy.

Introducing Your Landing Pages with End Screens

Adding an end screen to your video means ending with a call-to-action. Whether you want to prompt your viewers to subscribe to your channel, like your Facebook Page, or check out some more videos, end screens are the best way for you to achieve your goal.

To add end screens, just go to **'Video Manager'** and find the specific video you wish to add an end screen to. From the drop-down menu below your video, click on **'End Screens & Annotations'.** Make sure that the 'End Screen' tab is the one that's selected before you continue.

Important: You will be allowed to create an end screen only if your video is longer than 25 seconds, as the end screen is placed in the final five to twenty seconds of the video.

To create an end screen, you have three options to choose from:

1. The first option is to choose <u>a ready template</u> for your end screen. These predefined themes have all of the elements that an end screen should have, and are a very convenient way for YouTubers to ask for more engagement. Just choose the one that you find to be the most attractive, and then further customize it to fit your needs.

2. The second option is to make your <u>end screen from scratch</u>. This obviously requires a lot more work than the previous option, but it is also the best way to ensure that your brand will be presented in the best way possible. Here is where you can get really creative (or hire someone else to do it for you) and find the elements that will suit your video the most. To add an element, just click **'Add Element'** select the ones you want to add (you are allowed 4 elements max), fill in the details, and then finish by clicking **'Create Element'**. When selecting

the elements, keep in mind that one of them has to be a video (or a playlist).

3. The third option is to simply <u>import the end screen from another video</u> of yours.   If some of your videos include end screens, you can easily import one from there. Just click on **'Import from Video'** and then select the posted video. In the end, you will also have the option to edit the selected elements.

Generate Leads via Search

When it comes to YouTube (and Google in general) searches, the contextual keyword phrases are, without a shred of doubt, at the core of the queries. With that in mind, you can just imagine how detailed and well-explained description can help you rank high, not only on YouTube but on web searches as well.

Obviously, the longer your description is the higher your chance for getting discovered. However, long descriptions are more than just a bunch of long-tail keywords. When writing your video descriptions, make sure to make it as in-depth as possible, and include many different variations of your relevant keywords. By doing so, you may come up with something new and catch attention for some phrases that you didn't even use, which is pretty amazing.

While lengthy descriptions are great for recognition, what's more important is that first couple of lines that are shown without clicking on the 'Show More' button. Also, make sure to include the URL to your website so you can drive traffic there as well. But don't just copy and paste it. It is recommended that you add a UTM parameter to the link so you can track the clicks generated by the video. To make the link clickable, include **https://** so your viewers can be redirected to your website with a single click.

Marketing on Instagram

Even if your photos are of high quality and your posts are visually stunning, that alone will not bring you marketing success on Instagram. Just like with any other platform, promoting your brand on Instagram requires putting in a lot of work and knowing some techniques that will make you really stand out and slay the competition.

If your Instagram account is picture pretty but you still struggle to spread awareness and get some engagement from your followers, it is obvious that you need to find some new techniques to boost your following and get some interaction started. Read on to see what you can do to improve your Instagram marketing.

Taking Advantage of Instagram Stories

Most small businesses rely on posting pictures, overwhelming the audience with hashtags, and then waiting for someone to respond. Which is great, if you have been doing that for a while and already have an established audience. But if you are a small fish hoping to swim with the big sharks, then you need some big tactics in order to survive. Taking advantage of Instagram stories is one of those tips.

Although they are considered to be the new kid on the block – arrived in 2017 – Instagram Stories play a huge part in the marketing strategies of many businesses. Thanks to their ephemeral nature, these posts have really made a breakthrough.

So, what is Instagram Stories? Instagram Stories is a feature on Instagram that allows you to post images and videos that will remain visible on your account for up to hours. After that, they simply vanish into thin air. Whether you are planning to post a fun and upbeat short video or a business-focused photo, your business can definitely find value in this feature.

How Often is Too Often?

The greatest fact about this feature is that it will not get your account penalized for posting too often. In fact, you can post as many stories as you like on a daily basis. And because of the fact that these posts live only one day (as long as they are not highlighted, of course), they are shown in chronological order and there aren't any priorities on the feed. However, that doesn't mean that these posts are any less valuable than the regular ones. They are just as affected by the Instagram algorithm as any other post. However, with Instagram Stories, the frequency of your posts doesn't affect the number of people that will see the stories.

But, keep in mind that if you post too often you might look a bit spammy, and your followers may even decide to mute the posts from your account. There isn't really a secret to how often you should post. Keep in mind that posting too often requires a lot of time, effort, and management involved. While some companies have higher engagement if they post 10 stories per day, only you can decide whether you have that connection with your audience or not. Just know that once you establish the frequency of your stories, your followers will expect a continuance.

If you are a small business just getting into the waters of Instagram marketing, don't go overboard with this feature. Posting one story a day (or only a couple per week) may be the optimal frequency for achieving the goal of your business.

Posting Stories for Your Business

Just like with your regular Instagram posts, the Instagram Stories should also be engaging, informational, appealing, and promotional. But unlike with regular posting, the quality standard for Instagram Stories is pretty low. This gives you the opportunity to show your audience the raw, unpolished side of your business. It is also allowed to be a bit more relaxed or even goofy.

Many businesses have managed to drive engagement with this more natural side of promoting their brand. Using Instagram Stories is an essential tactic for many, so make sure to make it a part of your marketing strategy. Don't have any ideas on how to start your Story? Here are the most popular ways that businesses use this amazing feature for:

Promote Your Products or Services

The best thing about Instagram Stories is that it allows the audience to get a real and more natural feeling about your products or services. With a single 'tap', you can post a raw photo of your product that your customers will appreciate. Have a new product launched recently? Fill your Stories with different-angle photos of the product, photos of people using that product, or photos of your product in various environments. Just don't forget the call-to-action at the end, and you see how engaged your followers can be.

Behind the Scenes Look

To bring more authenticity to your content and invite your customers to take a peek at what's going on in your company during business hours, posting some behind-the-scenes content is probably the best way to achieve that. This is perfect for business of all sizes, as well. For instance, your small pastry shop can post a photo of your new pie and another behind-the-scenes photo of your employee making the pie. Or a large real estate company could take its audience around a new property that they have recently announced. There are endless possibilities of how this feature can be used.

Build an Engaged Community

Instagram Stories are usually posted with the purpose to encourage more followers to participate in the conversation. And since these posts are deleted from your feed after 24 hours, you shouldn't think too much about the lighting, the camera position, or about polishing the photo. This is the perfect chance for you to show your relaxed side and post light-hearted content that will make your follower's day and inspire them to become engaged.

People like honesty and genuineness. Showing

them this side of yours by, for example, posting a short video of your team dancing to their favorite tune while out for a post-work drink, may be just the thing your brand needs to keep your followers coming back for more.

Run a Takeover

An Instagram Story takeover means having segments with regular guests to bring some more consistency to your business Instagram account. You can do this with members of your team, or you can even partner up with another business to swap your stories for a day. This will bring variety to your content and inspire your audience to engage with your posts.

Features to Use

To use Instagram Stories as a part of the marketing strategy of your business, there are some features that you can make use of in order to present your brand in the best light, and get the most engagement from your followers.

Location and Hashtag Stickers

When the stickers were first introduced in 2017, they were nothing but a fun way to share your stories with your followers. But thanks to the new functionalities that Instagram has added, stickers are now as useful as they are fun, which makes them perfect for businesses to use when sharing a rawer side of their brand with the audience. The best of these functionalities are the ability to search Instagram Stories by hashtag and location.

Adding a Location

Adding a location sticker to your Instagram Stories can be of huge importance for your business, because by searching Instagram Stories by location in the Explore page, users can come across your Instagram Story and may even discover your brand that way.

To add a location, tap the sticker button and click on the **'Location'** option. A list of nearby locations will appear. Select the right one, and add your post. By tapping on the sticker, you can customize it by changing its color, etc.

Adding a Hashtag

Adding a hashtag to your Instagram Stories is just as simple. Just tap on the hashtag sticker, write your hashtag, and that's it. You can easily resize these stickers by expanding or pinching with two fingers.

Important: If you want your Stories to be seen by the public, make sure to set your account to Public. That way, when a user tags a hashtag in their Stories, or searches Instagram Stories by location, your Stories will come up.

Links

Adding clickable links to your Instagram Stories is a pretty big deal, as it will allow you to drive traffic to your website, YouTube channel, other social media platforms or another landing page that is relevant for your business.

Adding a Link

To add a link, you first have to have your video or photo taken. Next, click on the 'link' button at the top. You will be taken to a page where you will be prompted to enter (or paste) the URL to your landing page. When you're all set, just click **'done'** and that's it.

Adding a Call-to-Action

Keep in mind that your link will not be visible on the photo or video unless your followers swipe up the **'see more'** button. That being said, you can see how having this button will not be enough to entice your audience to click it and reveal the link.

Since the link button isn't as obvious as you'd want it to be, you have to let your audience know that they are supposed to take an action. Adding a call-to-action is the best way to do it. Call your users out by using appealing text or even arrow to get their attention.

Tagging

Tagging can also be a great way for you to redirect your followers to another landing page, and it can be your powerful weapon for driving traffic.

For instance, if you are running a contest, an influencer campaign, or even if you are planning a takeover, tagging other accounts can be of great importance for your overall marketing strategy.

Polls

Customers love feeling important, so asking their opinion on something can make them feel more valuable and will, in turn, result in increased engagement on their side. Including poll questions is a great way for you to include your customers in making decisions.

For instance, post an Instagram Story with a photo of two of your newest products, and create a poll where your audience can vote to let you know which product they want to see on discount first, or something of that sort.

To add your polls, take a photo or video, open the **'Stickers'** menu and click on the **'Poll'** sticker. Next, simply write your question and customize the choices. Now, post your story and wait to hear what your followers think.

Whether it is to see what your customers think of a certain product, crowdsource new ideas, or simply to post fun content for the sake of entertainment, the poll sticker gives your business many beneficial choices for your marketing strategy.

Countdown Stickers

Countdown stickers are a great way for you to emphasize the importance of taking an action in regard to an upcoming sale or discount that is about to end. Also great for announcing new product launches, adding a sticker that counts the remaining time is a perfect opportunity for you to send your customers a reminder in order to generate more results.

To add a countdown sticker, just tap the **'Stickers'** button, select the **'Countdown'** option, and add the details for your countdown.

Instagram Stories Highlights

As previously mentioned, highlighting Instagram Stories means giving your Story a permanent life that will not be deleted after 24 hours. Instagram Stories Highlights are an incredibly valuable feature that will allow your business to curate your content easily, in order to showcase those photos or videos that you want your audience to see first.

The best thing about these Highlights is that you can group them together by a topic or a theme, and make them a permanent part of your feed; until you decide to delete them, of course.

The Instagram Stories Highlights are displayed right under your bio and act as completely stand-alone Stories when a user clicks on them to view.

To add an Instagram Story Highlight, go to your profile and click on the **'Story Highlights'** found under your bio. Tap the **'+'** button, select the Story you wish to highlight, and click **'Next'**. Then you can simply choose a cover photo for your story and give it a name. Click **'Add'** or **'Done'** (depending on your device), and voila. Your story has now a permanent spot on your feed.

Driving the Best Results with Carousel Posts

Since they first appeared in mid-2017, carousel posts have really made a difference in the way in which businesses attract their audience. Much more versatile than regular Instagram photo posts, carousel posts allow you to promote product lines in a better, much appealing light. This feature of combining multiple images or videos in a single Insta post will provide your business with the opportunity to send your followers a much clearer marketing message.

Creating Carousel Posts

To create a carousel post, start by tapping the '+' sign, as you would normally do when adding an image. Once you do that, you will see a **'Create Multiple'** sign of stacked squares. Click on it. Scroll down your list of images or videos and select the ones you want to combine in a single post. You can select anywhere from 2 to 10 files. Click **'Next'**.

On the next screen that appears, you will have the option to **apply filters** and edit your images before posting. Keep in mind that any chosen filter will be applied to all of the selected images for the post. To edit the images individually, just tap on the image that you wish to apply filters to and choose the **edit** option. Once you are done, click on **'Done'**. If you want to reorder your images, just tap and hold the image you wish to change the order of, and then drag it to the desired spot.

After selecting and editing your images, you will be prompted to add your caption, just as you would in a regular post. And that's it. Just tap the **'Share'** button and your carousel post can be shared with your audience.

You can share portrait, landscape, and square formats in carousel posts, however, you are allowed to choose only one photo format per post.

The Uses

There are many different ways in which your business can turn these carousels posts to its advantage. These are some of the best uses that businesses have found multi-image posts to be beneficial for:

New Product Line Launches

Whether you want to promote your new eyeshadow line or your pet care business, sharing several photos of your new photo line is the best way not only for attracting your followers to click on your post and check out the new products, but also perfect for making more sales.

Does your product come in different colors? Carousel posts would be the perfect way to let your audience know that there is the perfect shade for everyone.

Capturing Multiple Features

Have a new product that is multi-functional? The best way to show off its capabilities is to create a carousel post and include an image of each of its valuable features. For instance, if you are selling a cotton baby carrier that can be also used as a car seat cover, a nursing cover, or a cute poncho for the mom, the best promoting strategy would be to capture all of these functions and combine it together in a single post. A short, fast-forwarded video of a mom transforming the carrier into its other functions would be the cherry on top.

Walking Through Step-by-Step Tutorials

The carousel post is perhaps best used when providing step-by-step tutorials of how something is done. For instance, if you want to share a recipe where the main ingredient is your organic coconut oil, this use will be your best strategy. Just divide the steps of the recipe into distinct sections, add an image (or a short video) for each of them, and then combine them into a single post to tickle the audience's taste buds and compel them to give it a try.

Behind-the-Scenes, How-It-Is-Made Photos

Insta Stories may be the perfect way to allow your followers to take a peek behind the scenes, carousel posts can also be a great way to share with your audience the making-of process of your product/service. Take a photo (or a short video) of each of the steps of the process of making your product, select them all for your carousel post, and let your audience see how your products are made.

324

Showcasing Before-And-After Sequences

This option works best if you are in the renovating or restoring business, and the concept here is pretty obvious. Share a photo of an old table from before, and then one of how the same table looks after your business has brought it back to life. But these sequences can have more meanings. Everyone can use this feature. Showcasing how your product works in real life can be one great way for this. And the best part? You can share up to 5 before-and-after sequences in a single post.

IGTV for Businesses

The moment that IGTV launched as the stand-alone video platform of Instagram, many businesses took the opportunity to take their Instagram marketing strategy to another level. And they were right. IGTV offers a new channel for your brand to promote itself, showcase your products and services, and grow your following. And the best thing about this is that, just like Insta Stories, IGTV is also a pretty relaxed space. You don't have to be obsessed with all the filters and polishing like you should be when sharing a high-class Instagram post. Think of IGTV as something between a regular post and Instagram Stories that can help you stretch the brand awareness even further.

Posting on IGTV

Posting on IGTV is pretty limitless. From product launches, how-to-tutorials, to sharing business info, so far, businesses have managed to gain success in many different ways on IGTV. The important thing – as with any other marketing strategy- is for you to be able to find a way to create value to your audience that will eventually result in value for your brand.

But first things first, before you can upload your content to IGTV you, obviously, need an IGTV account. So, download the IGTV app on your device, and sign up with your Instagram account. Then, click on the gear icon found in the upper right corner, and tap **'Create Channel'**.

Once your channel is created, you need to open it in order to upload content. To do so, click on your avatar from the main page. Then, click the '+' icon, and add your video to IGTV.

Keep in mind that if your video is not shown, it is probably because it is the wrong aspect ratio. For vertical videos, your aspect ratio should be a minimum 4:5 and a max of 9:16.

Next, simply add the title of your video and write a compelling description. Just like with YouTube videos, think about optimizing your IGTV content with relevant keywords. You can also add links, as your audience can be redirected to another landing page.

Finally, choose a thumbnail or add your own cover image. This image is what will be shown in the categories on IGTV, as well as up on your profile, so make sure it is visually compelling.

The aspect ratio for your cover photo should be 1:1.55 or 420 x 654 pixels.

2-Step Path to Success on IGTV

If you are already a pro in posting Instagram Stories, then beginning with IGTV shouldn't seem overwhelming or intimidating. Just think about IGTV as a simple step up from the Insta Stories. You can even use the same style and voice you use when sharing your Stories.

The only thing you need to consider here, is that IGTV, unlike Instagram Stories, means posting long-form content. That means that you will need some more time to shoot and edit your videos before actually publishing them. However, you can easily create a successful IGTV marketing strategy if you stick to these 2 golden rules:

#1: Be Comfortable with Vertical Videos

If editing video is not something you are comfortable doing, you will need some practice in order to post on IGTV. Why? Because unless you are shooting your video on your smartphone (most of them record vertically in 9:16 aspect ratio), you will need to edit the videos in post-production in order to get the aspect ratio right and be able to post on IGTV.

Lucky for you, you don't need to spend your money on expensive software or editing lessons. You can easily do this on your desktop. The first step you need to do is to download iMovie on your Mac desktop. Open it and create a new project. Rotate your video clip (if it is vertical) to avoid the tool adding black borders to the clip's sides, with the crop button. Then, edit your video as you see fit and save the file.

Don't forget to open the video in QuickTime before uploading it to your smartphone so you can rotate it back to being vertical again. Just go to '**Edit**' and rotate your video left or right.

Windows users can do the same using a tool like OpenShot, Movie Maker, or VideoPad.

Track the IGTV Analytics

IGTV is relatively new on Instagram, so it is still early for predicting how the audience responds to the uploaded content as well as for looking for certain patterns in their behavior. For that purpose, keeping a close eye on IGTV"'s analytics is the best way to stay on top of things and determine which content needs tweaking and which yields the best results.

IGTV's analytics can be accessed directly from the uploaded video. Just below the likes, views, and comments of your video, you can see it's retention rate, which shows you just how many of the viewers stuck with the content all the way through. But that's not all. If you open the drop-down graph, you will see exactly when the viewers decided to swipe away. This can be extremely beneficial as it is a great indicator of the performance of your videos. For instance, if most people decided to drop off after 15 minutes of watching, that can be a clear sign that your video shouldn't be that long. Having the analytics in mind, you can further edit or even reshot your videos in order to provide more value to your potential customers.

Your Influencer Marketing Strategy

Unless you have no social media account and aren't particularly interested in spending time online, chances are, you are pretty familiar with the term *influencer*. Influencers, as the name itself suggests, are those individuals who have managed to influence other people with their actions, position, knowledge, etc.

Influencers can be found throughout history, although when you hear this term today, it is unlikely that the topic is about Martin Luther King influencing with his civil right movement or Isaac Newton with his invaluable scientific discoveries. Influencers, in the modern sense of the word, are social media users who have the power to affect (or change entirely) someone's purchase choice thanks to their established credibility in a specific industry.

So, what is *influencer marketing* and how does it work? Influencer marketing is an inexpensive and highly effective strategy to grow your business on social media. It generally includes a brand partnering up with a popular Instagrammer (influencer) with the purpose of promoting their products/services. The influencer already has a large audience, and by promoting the brand's products, his/her followers will be persuaded to make a purchase. It's a simple trick that seems to be working like a charm.

Influencer marketing is a very popular strategy for spreading brand awareness and growing your following, as it breaks the traditional barriers of marketing and allows you to reach your customers through a source that they actually trust. So, when an influencer posts a picture of them trying a certain product or service, it doesn't seem as staged as having a celebrity promoting your brand, for instance, but it comes across as if their audience received a genuine recommendation from a friend.

Despite the fact that you can implement an Influencer Marketing strategy on almost any social media platform, it is highly recommended to give this journey a try on Instagram, as it is the best platform for social action.

Did you know? 67% of all marketers are already promoting their brand with influencers.

The Cost

Now that I've managed to tickle your imagination and got you thinking about giving Instagram Influencer Marketing a try, you must be wondering what that means for your budget. Influencer Marketing, just like the influencers themselves, really comes in all sizes. So, you can only imagine how the marketing rates vary. If you are looking to find an influencer who has over 100k followers, obviously, you have to be ready to pay a pretty substantial price. According to a 2018 report, some influencers even charge from $5000 to $10000 per one post. However, the common range is from $250 to $1000.

Keep in mind, though, that there are many factors that can determine the price of Influencer Marketing, and in the end, influencers with huge following may not even bring success to your business.

Micro-Influencer Marketing

If you are thinking about giving up on the idea of Influencer Marketing because of your tight budget, wait before you skip to the next chapter. To cash in on the influencer trend, you don't necessarily need to have thousands of dollars to spend. For your business, Micro-Influencer Marketing may be just what you need to reach to potential customers.

Micro influencers are those influencers who don't have hundreds of thousands of followers on their Instagram account, but they do have a smaller (micro) audience that is super engaged.

Now, micro can be anywhere from 1,000 to 100,000 followers. It all comes down to what kind of audience you want to be introduced to and what you are looking from an influencer.

The great thing about these micro-influencers is that unlike regular Instagram influencers who have attained a celebrity-like status, micro-influencers, come across as regular customers who can be super relatable and easy to trust. This is a great perk for small businesses as these influencers usually retain a higher engagement rate.

So, which type of influencer would be a better fit for your business? A celebrity-like individual who lives an almost-fairytale-like life, or a popular but trustworthy person who can recommend your products to about 5,000-15,000 people, giving a more genuine consumer message?

Want to know the best part about Micro-Influencer marketing? Most of these influencers do not promote products or services for money, but for free samples and gifts. Some of them also charge based on the leads or the sales that the sponsored post results in. It all depends on your marketing goal, your budget, and what you are trying to get out of this marketing strategy.

Why Your Business Needs It

With most businesses taking advantage of this popular marketing strategy, you really cannot afford to pass on an opportunity like this. If you're still wondering whether your business really needs this, let me tell you – it most certainly does. Instagram Influencer Marketing can be a real game-changer for your brand and will help your business row on many levels:

Increasing Brand Awareness

If you are a relatively new business, then your whole strategy should be based on building brand awareness in these initial stages. Teaming up with an influencer who already has the power to persuade their loyal fanbase what's good and what's not, can be a great way to present your products/services to a larger group of people. Think about it. If you team up with 3 influencers and have each of them post about a certain product of yours, you will have way more people looking at your products than you could have with 300 posts shared on your account.

Driving Sales

Influencer marketing is a great opportunity for you to drive more sales. Why? Because these influencers already have an engaged audience that is influenced by the things they do and want to buy the products they use. If played the right way, this can turn out to be the only marketing strategy you'll ever need. Take the watch company Daniel Wellington for an example. They solely depend on Instagram Influencer Marketing in order to drive sales. In 4 years, they have managed to achieve annual revenue of an incredible $220, mostly thanks to this Instagram marketing strategy.

How? Instead of simply spreading brand awareness, they were more concerned with driving more sales. They offered each influencer a free watch for a sponsored post. The influencers, then, gave a discount of 10-20 percent through a limited promotional code, to those followers who wanted to buy a watch. This worked great for both sides because the influencers were not just posting an advertisement, but they were also providing value to their followers by giving them a really cool discount.

Building Excitement for New Launches

What better way to get people excited about a new launch than having a popular Instagrammer promoting it? The ultimate strategy here is to offer influencers free products that are yet to be launched that they should promote on Instagram (and get to keep, of course). That way you will not only market your products/services before they even hit the stores, but also position them as something cool through the excitement that the influencer is about to share with their fans.

Encouraging the Use of Your Branded Hashtag

If you have a branded hashtag and you want to get more people to use, then turning to an influencer for help can be just the thing you need. By having the influencer post with your #hashtag, their audience will be introduced to it and encouraged to jump on that bandwagon and use it in their posts, too. This will eventually result not only in increasing brand awareness but driving more traffic and sales as well.

Finding the Right Influencers for Your Brand

Now, to the trickier part. How do you actually find the right Instagrammer so that your business can benefit from their influence? Whatever your goal, the three things that you need to check before contacting an influencer are:

#1: Their Engagement

If an influencer has a lot of engagement, it means that their influence is pretty strong, and their followers are paying attention to their posts. Check their profile and see how their posts are performing. If the engagement rate is somewhere between 2 and 4%, that means that they have a solid audience who is engagement. A rate of 4 to 6 percent is excellent, while posts with an engagement rate higher than 15 or 20% are considered to be viral.

#2: The Quality of their Audience

If you are selling healthy and organic drinks and smoothies, it is obvious that you'd want to partner up with an influencer whose audience is interested in weight-loss, healthy living, nutrition, regular exercise, etc. Your influencer should have a following that is similar to your ideal audience, in order for your Instagram Influencer Marketing campaign to be successful.

#3: The Number of Followers

Okay, the number of followers isn't necessarily the best metric to look at, however, in some cases, teaming up with huge influencers can be a great strategy if you want to let the world know your brand exists. Just keep in mind that, in most cases, the rate of engagement decreases as the number of followers grows.

Finding the perfect influencer for your brand can be a bit of a challenge, but the most important thing is to be sure just what you are looking for. For instance, if you have a goal to just spread brand awareness, the important metrics to look for in an influencer would be traffic and reach. However, if you want to increase your engagement rate, then teaming up with a micro-influencer who has a smaller but more engaged audience would be the right tactic.

And if you are wondering what your approach should be like, that depends solely on you. What are you ready to offer and what is your budget? Craft a good and appealing proposal before actually contacting the influencer. You can offer a flat rate, a price per sale, free products, a very generous discount, whatever you think it's best for your brand.

Marketing on Twitter

Although Twitter has gained the reputation for being the noisy, microblogging site, it can actually be a great marketing tool for businesses of all sizes. But with over 500 million Tweets being sent each day, you can see that getting the right kind of attention in the middle of all that noise can be tricky.

If you've already started your Twitter marketing journey, chances are, you're already well aware that being so communication-oriented, Twitter is a social media platform that deserves a somewhat more customized marketing strategy. In order for you to be able to get through to your audience on the busiest network, this chapter will provide you with some tips and tricks for your business to succeed.

Promoting in 280 Characters

When Twitter decided to make the change from 140 to allowing 280 characters per post, that was probably the biggest social media shift since the transformation that Facebook made to its news feed a few years back.

But even though that it's doubled in size and may seem like a lot, once you start typing with the purpose of promoting your product in the best way possible, you will see that you cannot fit everything you want to say. And compared to the thousands of characters allowed on Facebook, Twitter can seem quite frustrating at times.

Here are some tips on how to make the most out of this character limit, and how to make your brand's Tweets engaging:

Don't Use Shortened Words – Many people use shortened words (think *u* instead of *you*, or *4* instead of *for*, etc.) to be able to fit their thoughts into the 280-character limit. But while this may seem like a smart thing, keep in mind that abbreviations give an unprofessional feeling. Your sentences should be clear. If your followers cannot

343

read and understand the sentence at first glance, you will definitely lose them.

Use Characters – You may come across as unprofessional if you spell the word *great* as *gr8,* but using allowed characters is totally approved. Why waste your characters to say *percent*, when % will say the same thing with a single character?

Use Shorter Words Instead – Instead of cutting your word short, use their shorter counterparts instead. For instance, if you want to say *enormous*, stick to its shorter synonym *big* to explain the same thing in fewer characters. Just be sure to use the right words, as not all synonyms send the same message.

Make Every Word Count – Avoid using filler words. Make sure that every word you type in makes an impact and shows and actions, and avoid empty words such as *that*.

Do Not Skip on Punctuation - Do not be tempted to skip the comma or the period for the sake of the character count. Punctuation matters and run-on promotions are definitely not going to attract your audience.

Get to the Point - Try not to mince your words but get right to the point. This will not only save you a lot of characters but posting clear sentences attract people's attention more.

Try not to Break Up Your Tweets – Dividing your Tweets in order to continue your thought may be the only way in which you can completely make your point, but keep in mind that not everyone will see both of your Tweets. Many of your followers may actually end up getting confused and not understand what it is that you're talking about.

Twitter Advanced Search for Getting More Leads

Lead generation is of incredible value for any business, as it is all about collecting info from potential customers and passing them onto your team, in order to incorporate the features your

345

customers are looking for into your products/services with the purpose of driving more sales.

However, with over 6,000 tweets that happen per second, you can see how barraging through the Twitter clutter can be overwhelming. Finding specific info in the middle of all that noise can be next to impossible. For that purpose, Twitter has provided us with a great built-in tool called the *Advanced Search* that will save you tons hours of time and wasted energy.

If you want to get the most out of this tool for the sake of your brand's lead generation goals, follow the next few tips:

Explore Keywords and Hashtags

The most obvious way to use the Advanced Search is for exploring keywords and hashtags that are relevant for your business. By doing so, you will be able to reveal an entire community of people who are talking about your field. For instance, if you are

346

a healthy drinks company, you would probably want to explore keywords such as *diet* or hashtags like *#weightloss* or *#health.* This will help you to follow real-time conversations that are centered around a certain topic that is related to your business.

Target Your Searches by Location

Whether you have a local thrift shop or are running an international business, it is always the best strategy to connect with your audience on a local level. By listening to the conversations of your potential customers from a specific location, you will be able to gather solid info about what they're buying habits are. Why? Because people in Los Angeles and Dallas may be talking about different needs. Narrowing your search by location will help you make a more continuous relationship with your customers.

Search by Sentiment

Once you start using the Advanced Search option, you will see that there are many different filters that can be applied to your searches, which is of great value when you are looking for high-class leads. One of the best options available is *searching by sentiment.*

Searching by sentiment will allow you to refine your search and check out only the positive things that are said about your business, or the other way around. This can be of huge importance if you are looking to reach out to an ambassador of your brand, as you are more likely to find the most loyal customers when you are only going through the positives.

But searching only for the negatives can also lead to growing your success. By determining what the main complaints of your customers are, you will be able to pinpoint exactly what needs to be modified in order to decrease the bad experiences associated with your brand.

Answering Questions

348

Similarly to searching by sentiment, you can also use the Advanced Search tool to look for questions. The question filter will help you find specific concerns or issues that Twitter users have within your field. Finding the right questions that you can give your answer to will help you reach out to more customers. You just need to explore the types of questions that people ask – whether about your business in particular or another related subject – and position your brand as the main authority of that particular subject. This will result in more followers, and eventually, more paid customers.

Hosting a Twitter Chat

A *Twitter Chat* is the place where Twitter members who share similar interests, come together at a previously determined time in order to communicate and share their thoughts on a specific topic with the use of a designated hashtag for every contributed tweet. There is a host (or a moderator) who is in charge of asking the questions to the participants, and it is the one who encourages the

349

interaction. Twitter chats last about an hour on average.

Why You Should Participate

A Twitter Chat can be a very powerful tool for the marketer. When hosted regularly (once a week), Twitter Chats can provide your brand with the chance to connect with your community in a better way. By discussing issues that everyone is affected by, you can share tips and ideas with your community, and grow your circle and strengthen the connection with your audience in return.

Here is what your brand can get out of hosting a Twitter Chat:

- You get to create brand awareness by having a strong, engaging presence

- You can get people talking about you with your hashtag

- Your audience may have a good time and share the chat with others

350

- You will create a conversation among people with similar interests

- By having your hashtag appear on the stream, it may attract other people and you may end up with more followers

- You can meet other professionals, collaborators, and other people that can be valuable to your business

- You will help people learn about your community

Finding the Right #Hashtag

The hashtag is the single most important part of Twitter posts. It is a relevant word preceded by '#' that categorizes messages or helps users search for tweets. If you are already active on Twitter, then you probably know what hashtags mean for this network.

The hashtag in the Twitter Chat has the same meaning. It stands for the name of the chat, and it is mentioned in every Tweet, It is also how users can discover your chat.

You may think that coming up with a hashtag is simple, but the truth is, this is the hardest part. Why? Because there already are tons of chats out on Twitter already, and you need to come up with one that hasn't been used. It also has to be short (since it has to be mentioned in every Tweet), but also simple and clear.

The hashtag is what can make or break your chat, so choose wisely. The most popular chats are the ones that use the most obvious chats. For instance, *#blogchat* is a chat about bloggers.

The first part of the hashtag is usually the brand's name, and the end of the hashtag, the word *chat* is added so that users know what the hashtag is about. Your hashtag has to reflect your brand and has to be unique. For instance, if you're a wooden toy manufacturer, your hashtag may be *#woodentoyschat* or *#thenameofyourbrandchat* or whatever makes your chat stand out and helps people discover it.

Scheduling Your Chat

Your Twitter Chat must have a scheduled time and date in order for users to know when to partake. But you cannot simply set the time that works for you without making some prior considerations first. The most important thing that you need to think about is when your audience will actually be able to participate. For instance, you cannot choose to host the chat in the morning for Europe and expect to receive engagement from Pacific Time as well. If your audience is in different time zones, you need to find the perfect balance and choose the time that will work for the majority of your audience.

Also, don't forget to think about the time when your audience is most active on Twitter. This cannot be done without some trial and error, so feel free to experiment until you find the perfect timing for your Twitter Chat.

Making a Plan

You will need to create a good plan in order to make your chat successful. The most common mistake that businesses make is they tend to make the topic too specialized and fail to receive participation from users that are outside of their niche. Of course, keep your topic brand-focused, but don't make it to boring to encourage other people to join.

Once you decide on the topic that the chat will focus on, get more specific and write down the details. What questions are you planning to ask? The general rule of a thumb is for the host to ask about 6 - 10 questions, but this, obviously, depends on your business and your preferences. Since the Twitter Chat has a Q&A format, your questions should be composed in a compelling and engaging way to get more answers from the participants.

Make sure to also have a few back-up questions prepared that you will be able to throw in depending on the direction of the chat. Make a plan, but don't be afraid to go with the flow. This will give your conversation a more natural course and will encourage your chatters to come back for more.

Finding the Guests

A Twitter Chat can be a great way for you to share your expertise and ask for feedback from your audience. But if your plan is to be at the heart of the conversation every time, things may get quite boring after a chat or two. For that purpose, bringing in guests who will share their thoughts is a great way for you to stay within your area of expertise and still reach new audiences.

So, take your time to do some research in order to find the movers and shakers in your field, and ask them to join you for a chat. Let them know how they can also benefit from the chat to avoid being turned down: they will get more visibility, they will be able to promote themselves and their work, share some stats with them to prove your point, etc.

Hosting with Success

As a great host, you will need a certain chat format to stick to. If you are planning to run a 60-minute chat, try this format to yield the best results:

#1: Welcome Community Members

Welcome your community members and everyone who wishes to participate at the beginning of your chat. Ask them all to introduce themselves and share a few details. Allow them about 3 minutes for this.

#2: Introduce the Format of the Chat

Most chats are prefaced with the first question as Q1. The users will respond with A1 as the first answer, and so on. This is a great way to avoid getting confused and know exactly which question a certain answer refers to.

When asking questions to your guests, do not forget to use the '@' sign when replying. For instance, *@yourguest'sname, why do you think that is?*

#3: Retweet

Make sure to retweet your guest's answers, as well as your own questions. Also, check out the responses that are being shared by your community the most, and make sure to retweet those, too.

#4: Plan for Your Next Question

It's recommended to ask the next question not before 6 minutes and not longer than 10 minutes after starting the chat. The point is to plan your minutes wisely, so you have enough space not only to ask the questions, but also to respond.

#5: Let Your Guests Ask

If you have some time on your hands, allow your guests a couple of minutes to ask your guest some questions.

#6: Wrap It Up

About 2-3 minutes before the end, ask your guests if there is something they wish to end or promote.

#7: Sign Out!

End your chat by making your special announcements and reminding everybody of your next chat. If you already know who your guest will be, make sure to let your guests know.

Who Said What? If you are having a hard time keeping up with your guest's answers, you may want to seriously consider viewing your chat outside of Twitter. For instance, http://tweetchat.com/ is a great platform that allows you to only view the tweets for a particular hashtag, so this is a great opportunity to avoid getting confused by other tweets in your stream.

The Ultimate Dos and Don'ts of Twitter Marketing

You may think that your number one strategy should be making each and every one of your tweets about highlighting your products, but the line between successfully promoting and spamming is rather a thin one. The balance here is delicate, and if you try too hard to get people's attention, you might end up losing your existing followers. The beauty of Twitter – which other social media platforms lack of – is that it is the number one network for conversational promoting. That means that you get to promote your brand without even promoting it.

By being connected to the right people, talking to your audience the right way, and providing nothing but value (and a dash of entertainment, obviously) you will create a killer marketing strategy that will get you across the street from your goal.

Play your promoting Twitter game by these rules to avoid sounding overly promoting and provide content that your Twitter followers will want to talk about:

DO Follow the Right People

Most businesses make a lethal mistake by following as many people as they possibly can, but that will only lower your credibility and make you look like a fraud. Following a huge group of people hoping that you will receive follows in return leads to nothing more but cluttered stream that people will find hard to follow. If you want to receive the best level of engagement, make sure that you follow only those people that truly matter to your business and that will receive the most value from your contents.

DON'T Auto-Follow Your Followers

Be smart about your followers. Do not auto-follow everyone who becomes a fan of yours. Avoid using an auto-follow ap that will automatically make you a follower of your followers. Why? Because those profiles that auto-follow their audience are easy to spot thanks to their follower/following ration. Such a disbalance will present you s a spammer, which may cost you many followers.

DO Use the Right Keywords

Thorough keyword research will show you which phrases your business is most likely to benefit from by mentioning them in the tweets. Make sure to use your keywords wisely in order to improve your Twitter's visibility.

DON'T Spam People Who Are Talking about These Keywords

Slapping people with links to discounts or promotional codes whenever you hear the name of your product will not drive more sales. Quite the contrary. People on Twitter hate being bothered, so make sure not to come out of the woodwork promoting your brand whenever a user uses a relevant keyword. The keywords should be mainly used as suggestions and guides, not a reason for you to hit a sales pitch to every Twitter user who is interested in the relevant keywords.

DO Talk about Your Brand

Sure, Twitter may be all about the conversation, but don't forget why you're there. Take the time to talk about your brand and introduce your audience with the new launches, features, updates, and other important business-related stuff that your followers can benefit from.

DON'T Talk Only about Your Brand

The key to running a successful Twitter campaign is to find the perfect balance between promoting your brand and communicating with your followers. Of course, this ratio is not set in stone and is different for every business. Trial and error is ultimately the best tactic to find what works for you best, however, marketing experts say that the perfect ratio is 1-2 promotional tweets out of 10 tweets.

DO Find Interesting Topics to Talk about

Introducing appealing topics to discuss with your audience will increase their engagement and even bring you more followers. Go for a new topic each day. Try to find some news that is related to your business, or talk about some of your newest techniques, etc. Just make sure that the discussion will interest your followers.

DON'T Be Too Corporate

Keep in mind that your followers are not on Twitter to talk about your brand. Avoid sharing corporate content that will make you no fun to be around. You are allowed to share company business from time to time, but make sure to bring entertainment back to your Twitter. It's all about the balance.

Marketing on LinkedIn

What will make users mute your posts on other social media platforms and crown you as *boring* will help you establish your brand as an authority on LinkedIn. LinkedIn is the biggest B2B network where publishing press releases and important company info is not only expected but will also get you the right connections and help you grow a successful business.

LinkedIn usually gets a bump mainly because people don't really know how to use it. Since it is centered around business-related content and not holiday photos, many decide to write this platform off. But just because it seems harder to connect with people on LinkedIn, doesn't mean is not possible.

If you are a B2B business, then this is the platform you should definitely invest the most of your time and energy in. But if you think that LinkedIn is nothing more but a network where job seekers upload their resumes hoping to get employed, you cannot be more wrong. LinkedIn can be an invaluable marketing tool if used the right way.

So, don't give up on LinkedIn just yet if you don't know what to do with your company page. This chapter will teach you all there is to know about marketing your business on this platform.

Optimizing Your Page

You may have created your business page on LinkedIn with success, but that doesn't mean that your strategy will be successful. Your company page is the public listing of your company, both in the LinkedIn's on-site search, as well as on Google. In order to make sure that your page will be easy-to-find and at the top of the search results, you will have to optimize it first. Here are some optimization tips for better performance and generating more leads:

Check Your Company's Info

Check to see if your NAP (name, address, and phone number) is actually consistent with the info on other listings. By doing so you make sure that people can reach you easily. This may sound as too obvious, but you'd be surprise of the damage that a single dot or a wrong digit can do.

Use the Banner Image

Your banner image – best at 646 x 220 pixels – can be just the thing you need to define your brand and make it really stand out on LinkedIn. Of course, it is recommended to stay with your brand's recognition style and colors, however, add a little more value to your LinkedIn audience. For instance, have something like "Become Our Follower to Learn how to Manage Your Team" written, that will offer a tempting proposition to the LinkedIn users.

Use the Link Wisely

Most users add links on their business page that lead to their homepage. Don't waste precious space and opportunity to direct people to a better landing page and use this chance to capture emails or even send a personalized message to your visitors.

Link Your Profile to Your Page

Linking your personal LinkedIn profile to your business page can be of great value. Go to your personal page and click on **'Experiences'**. Under **'Company Name'**, add the name of your company.

Don't Shy Away from Keywords

Just like with any other social platform, the use of relevant keywords is also crucial for your marketing strategy on LinkedIn. Make sure to use the right phrases that are relevant for your business throughout the page, but pay close attention to how you're using them in your 'About' section.

Have Your Employees on Board

Nothing screams *healthy business* like having content employees. Make sure to encourage your team not only to like your company's LinkedIn page but also to share your content. There are no better brand ambassadors than the people that are employed by the business.

Promoting and Selling on LinkedIn

If you want to highlight initiatives or special products on LinkedIn, there is no better way to do it than by using *showcase pages.* Showcase pages are, in a way, similar to your business page. They are stand-alone pages where you can make your big announcements and introduce people with your newest product launches or services, announce special events, or any other kind of opportunity that your business may benefit from. Think of a showcase page as a valuable addition to your business page where you can share a particular part of your business and engage with your audience.

For instance, if your company has multiple smaller brands, you can use showcase pages and create a special place for each of your brands. Something like Facebook Groups, but in a much more specific, business-related way.

Businesses use showcase pages because they can:

Share Info about Their Brand. Unlike writing a short status update, showcase pages make it possible for you to share as much as info as you'd want your LinkedIn audience to be aware of.

Share Info only with Relevant People. People follow only those showcases that particularly interested. For instance, if someone is interested in one aspect of your business but not in something else that you do, they will most likely follow only the showcase that is relevant to them. This means that you will have a more targeted audience, and that you don't have to sell your brand as much as you should on your business page.

Increase Engagement. Having many showcase pages means having many opportunities for establishing communication with your well-educated LinkedIn audience.

Creating a Successful Showcase Page

Before even thinking about creating a Showcase Page, it is of crucial importance that you know that Showcase Pages cannot be simply unpublished. If you want to delete and completely deactivate the page, you have to contact LinkedIn and ask them to remove it. With that in mind, you need to pay close attention od why and how you are creating your showcase page.

A showcase page can only be created by the administrator of the company page. In order to do so, follow the next steps:

1. Go to your company page and open the drop-down menu that is found next to the **'Edit'** button. Select **'Create a Showcase Page'**.

2. Now, a Showcase Page pop-up window will appear. Click on the **'Get Started'** button.

3. Enter the relevant information like the name of your Showcase Page, and appoint an administrator for the page.

4. Click on **'Create Page'**. At this point, LinkedIn will show you what your page will look like. If you are not happy with the look, make some changes. If it looks good, jump to the next step.

5. Finally, click on the **'Publish'** button and you're Showcase Page will go Live in no time.

Starting a LinkedIn Group

A LinkedIn Group is very different from your business page, personal LinkedIn profile, or even your showcase pages. LinkedIn groups are not about promoting your brand nor about selling your products. At least not in the obvious sense of the word, that is. Groups are about having a place to discuss certain niche or topics with your community, in order to grow your audience and increase their engagement. So, you might not be able to sell your services there, but by learning about your audience, LinkedIn Groups provide you with the opportunity of actually improving the sales process.

Why Your Business Needs a LinkedIn Group

If you are wondering whether creating and managing a LinkedIn Group is worth your time and money, take a look at these benefits to see just what you can get out of these groups:

Establishing Expertise - If you are a B2B business owner, then a LinkedIn Group may be just what you need to establish your reputation as being one of the biggest experts in your industry. By taking a part in discussions, you get to show off with your knowledge.

Driving Traffic – By placing links that direct to your website or another sales page, you will get the chance to drive more traffic there.

Expanding Your Reach – By having a group where you will discuss certain topics with like-minded people, you will easily make new connections.

Understanding Your Community – Since you will be communicating with your community, you will have the chance to learn about their questions, concerns, thoughts, etc. first hand. This will create a great opportunity for you to shape your content and your services with the purpose of attracting new customers.

Sending Weekly Updates – Being the owner of a LinkedIn Group, you will get the chance to send weekly messages to everyone who follows your group. This can be a great way for you to make sure that your community is aware of the latest company information, product updates, new events, etc.

Setting Up Your Group

Your LinkedIn group can be set up in a jiffy. It will not take more than just a couple of minutes, and the process is pretty simple and straightforward. Just follow the next steps and you will have one up and running in no time:

1. Find **'Interests'** at the top of your page, click on it, and then hit **'Groups'** from the drop-down menu. The page with the Group Highlights will appear.

2. Select **'My Groups'** found at the top of the page.

3. Find **'Create a Group'** in the left sidebar and click on it.

4. Now, enter all of the relevant info about your group: the name of the group, description, summary, website URL, etc. Keep in mind that the relevant keywords play a huge role here as well, so make sure to be engaging and descriptive, but also tactical.

5. Next, upload your photo or log. This is optional, but highly recommended.

6. When creating your Group, you will have the option to choose whether you want it to be public or not. If you don't want the Group to be public, make sure that **'Unlisted'** is checked.

7. Accept the Terms of Service.

8. Finally, hit the **'Create Group'** button.

And that's it. Now, you are a proud owner of a LinkedIn Group.

Standard or Unlisted Group?

There are two options for your LinkedIn Group – you can choose it to be *standard* or *unlisted.*

In a Standard LinkedIn Group:

- The discussions will be shown in Google's search results

- The members of the Group can invite other LinkedIn users to join

In an Unlisted LinkedIn Group:

375

- The discussions will not be shown in search engine results

- Only the members of the group will be able to see the discussions

- Only the Group's administrator can invite (and approve) users to join the group

- A padlock icon will be shown to indicated that the group is unlisted

So, all in all, a standard group is an open, public group, and an unlisted group is closed, private group. Choosing the right one for your business is something that only you can do. They both have their pros and cons, but ultimately, it all comes down to what you are looking for.

For instance, an unlisted group may be a better option for you to control the membership, as well as to reduce spamming. However, these groups don't grow at the same pace as the standard ones do. Having an open group may be a better option if your business is new, as it will be visible for everyone to see and might help spread brand awareness.

Inviting Users to Join Your Group

The first thing that you need to do after successfully creating a LinkedIn Groups, is to find the group some members. To increase the membership of the group, you will have to invite others to join:

1. Click on **'Interests'** from the top of your page, and then choose **'My Groups'** from the drop-down menu.

2. Select your Group.

3. Click on **'Manage'** found at the upper right corner.

4. Choose **'Send Invitations'** from you're the left sidebar. A pre-written invitation will appear. Keep in mind that there is no way for you to customize the invitation, but you need to send it as is.

5. Click on **'In'** found next to the **'Connections'** text box, and select those people that you're connected with that you want to send the invitation to. Know that you will also have the option to invite other people to join, even if you are not connected to them. All you have to do is simply type their email address in the connection name box.

6. Finally, click on **'Send Invitations'**. The people you've invited will then get a notification at the upper right corner of their LinkedIn page or receive an email (if you've sent invitations to people who are not your connections on LinkedIn).

LinkedIn as a Content Platform

LinkedIn offers the opportunity for you the publish content in a long form. Even if you have (and successfully use) a website or a blog, publishing longer content on LinkedIn will not only help you

378

reach a more professional social network, but will also throw many other benefits your way:

- Your posts will become visible on your personal profile. This will further promote your brand as anyone who clicks on your professional profile on LinkedIn will be able to check out the post published by your brand.

- People that are not connected to your business can also see your post which creates a huge opportunity for brand recognition and increasing your audience.

- LinkedIn users can follow your published content, even if they do not choose to follow you.

- Every one of your connections will be notified about the published post, which only increases the probability that the people you're connected to will see the post.

- The chances for engaging with other professionals are significantly received, as readers can also like and comment on your posts.

Creating Your First Post

Your post can be easily created from your LinkedIn home page in just a few steps:

1. Click on **'Home'** at the upper left corner of your LinkedIn Page.

2. Select **'Write an Article'** from the top of your page.

3. Enter your title in the title area.

4. In **'Write Here'**, write (or paste) the content that you wish to publish.

5. Finally, click on **'Publish'** from the upper right corner.

Keeping It Professional

Since LinkedIn is a network for career-oriented and professional people, it is only understandable that you cannot post your content in the same style as you write your Insta captions. When posting on LinkedIn, you have to do it in a professional tone that will attract the attention not only of your connections but other LinkedIn members as well. Here are some tips that will help you write a successful LinkedIn post in a professional manner:

Solve Problems. Keep in mind that people want to know about what you do in order to solve some issues that they are dealing with. Make sure that your content will answer questions and solve problems. Your readers will appreciate if you guide them and teach, not post fluff.

Give Advice. Many young professionals who want to try themselves in your industry will appreciate having advice from experts. What are the things you wish you knew when you were starting out? Share some tips and educate.

Keep it Up-to-the-Point. Really long content makes people lose interest. Your LinkedIn posts should be between 500 and 800 words, so make sure not to publish longer content.

Respond to Comments. Make sure to respond to every comment. Your readers will appreciate that you value their opinion which will most likely encourage them to share your content.

Be Careful with the Links. Links can be included in your post, but only if they are part of the discussion and make links. Don't just drop links out of the blue as it will look unprofessional and spammy.

Use Rich Media. Adding some visual elements to your post will make it much more appealing. On LinkedIn, it is allowed to use images, presentation from SlideShare, as well as embed YouTube videos.

Once your post is published, do not forget to promote it. Make sure that you share a link to your post on your other social media platforms in order to grow your connections, increase awareness, and let your audience know that you are always working on something new.

Tips for Getting More LinkedIn Followers

Getting more people to like your company page on LinkedIn can feel like an impossible thing to achieve. But while attracting new followers can be somewhat a challenge, it is indeed possible.

Growing your following on LinkedIn comes down to two things:

1. Promoting your page on other platforms

2. Implementing some strategies to attract more people

And while the first point requires some commitment and effort on your side, I can definitely help you with the latter. Here are the ultimate tips that will help you increase the number of your LinkedIn followers:

- Create a badge for your LinkedIn page that will be placed on your website or blog. You can use the LinkedIn Plugin Generator for this purpose https://developer.linkedin.com/plugins

- Post regularly. According to LinkedIn, the most successful pages are the ones that post at least 20 times a month, so make sure that you update your community on a regular basis.

- Make sure to use the LinkedIn share buttons with your posts in order to encourage your readers to share your content.

- Share job opportunities postings on your LinkedIn business page. This is one of the main things that attracts the eye of the LinkedIn members, so make sure to take care of that.

- Be informative with your posts. The most successful posts are the ones that share the best information, so make sure to keep your followers updated with latest company news, product development, upcoming events, etc.

- Post at the BEST TIMES in order to improve your visibility and get the most engagement, which will, in turn, lead to growing your following. The rule of a thumb is to publish after business hours and in the mornings for the highest engagement rate.

- Make sure to include a link to your business LinkedIn page in the bio of your guest posts.

Marketing on Pinterest

Sill think that only Facebook and Instagram are the marketing platforms worth investing in? Well, think again. Did you know that a Pin is a hundred times more spreadable than a Tweet? Or that Pins live way longer than Facebook posts? Or that if your business takes the right approach, it can show its customers how to use your products/services in the most visually stunning way possible?

If you were attracted by Pinterest before but failed to wow your customers with your boards and pins, do not despair. Just because you haven't managed to draw the right attention from Pinners, doesn't mean that your marketing campaign on Pinterest is a vain attempt. This chapter will show you what have you been doing wrong and how to improve your strategy for growing your brand on Pinterest.

Quality Pins for More Saves

Saves, or formerly known as *repins,* mean saving something that was already pinned by someone.

The pins you create will have to attract people visually, in order to compel them to save them to their board. 80 percent of the content that is shared on Pinterest is Saves. The first tactic of your marketing campaign on Pinterest should be to abide by the 80/20 rule. What does that mean? That means that you should share 20% of your own content and save 80% of the things that have already been pinned. This is a huge marketing mistake that most small businesses make in the beginning, so make sure to save 4 other pins for every piece of content that you share on Pinterest.

But even though the larger chunk of your content on your board should be repins, you still have to figure out how to create and share your content in order to make other people save your Pins. After all, that is the whole point on Pinterest Marketing – getting people to save your content in order to promote your brand. And for that purpose, you need to focus on creating and sharing Pins of high quality.

Writing Your Pins

Even though Pinterest is considered to be a visual platform where a little attention is given to the captions and titles, the truth is, it is the description of your Pins that help people discover them in the first place. Think about it, if they are not actually typing something like *organic all-natural face cream* in the search bar, how on earth will your potential customers be able to find your face cream Pins?

Here is how you can write a compelling Pin:

Go for Longer Descriptions – Research shows that it is actually the Pins that have longer descriptions that actually get the most saves. So, if you want to get more repins and click-through rates, go slightly over 300 characters when describing your Pins.

Include a Call-to-Action – This is a no brainer. If you want your Pins to be saved, tell people to click through. Including a killer CTA in your description can really make a difference.

Use Keywords – Keep in mind that your audience finds your content by using keywords. Like *organic, all-natural, face cream.* Make sure to find the ones that are relevant for your Pins and incorporate them into your descriptions. Just make sure not to overdo it as your description has to make a sense.

Include a Link to your Website – Whether your website, blog, sales site, or another landing page, the point is to direct your audience where you want them to go with a clickable link.

Mention Others - When sharing someone else's content, be sure to thank them by mentioning them.

Only 75-100 characters of your description will be shown in the grid view of your Pin, so make sure to add the most important info at the beginning.

Things to Know about Hashtags:

Hashtags on Pinterest do not have the same meaning as they do on Twitter or Instagram. They will not help your Pins show in search results, nor will improve your visibility. Here, hashtags are used simply as a categorical symbol that you can add to your description in order to help other find similar things.

It's important to know that hashtags on Pinterest can actually have the contra effect sometimes. By having a hashtag that users can click on, you can actually take your potential Pinners away, without a point to return. If you end up using a hashtag, however, make it super unique.

Designing Your Pins

In order for your Pins to get saved, they need to be no less than visually stunning. But just because you need to add high-class imagery doesn't mean that you have to be a designer. Just follow the next three guidelines when creating your Pins, and repins are guaranteed:

Rely on Custom Imagery and Effective Colors

You may be tempted to purchase a beautiful stock photo to use for your Pins, but that would be a mistake. Stock photography doesn't yield the best results on Pinterest. Your Pins should be actionable, helpful, and visually compelling. Instead of reaching for a stock image, try out some super fun photo editing tools and get creative. If creativity is not particularly your strong suit, then think about hiring a graphic designer to do the images for you. However you decide to create your images, here is what you should know:

- Faceless images receive about 23 percent more saves that images with faces

- Red and orange Pins perform twice better than blue and multiple-colored Pins

- Pins with less-distracting background gain more traffic

- Simple design works the best

Include Text on Imagery with Overlays

Overlay is another super helpful element that your images should contain. This is great for clarifying the message that your Pin is trying to send as the overlay will improve the readability of the text.

Also, it's good to know that overlays can be quite beneficial when using them in embedded Pins outside of Pinterest (like on your website or blog).

Have Longer Images

When designing your image, make sure to choose 735 px to be the width. As for the length, you can make it as long as you'd like it to be. These longer images can help your content get easily spotted as they tend to really stand out on Pinterest boards.

Keep in mind that it is said that Pins with an aspect ratio of 2:3 or 4:5 receive the most traffic. But if you want to get more click-throughs, then the best hack is to simply include on tall and Pinnable image to be at the top of your blog post.

Determining the Pin Type

Many businesses make the mistake of not using all of the Pin types to their advantage, simply because they are unaware that there are actually more than one type out there. Besides the 'regular' save or repin, there are three more different Pins that you can use in order to increase your reach.

Rich Pins

Rich Pins are standard Pins that you can add some extra context to, in order to give your Pins some more character. These Pins include additional information that the Pinners find super beneficial. They, usually, can be found in 4 categories:

1. Recipe Pins – They attract Pinners with their list of ingredients, cooking times, etc.

2. Product Pins – They make the process of shopping easier thanks to their real-time prices and other product info

3. Article Pins – They show the author name, headlines, description of the story, etc.

4. App Pins – They feature an install button for downloading apps without even leaving Pinterest. This option is only available on iOS.

There are two millions of people who save Rich Pins on a daily basis, so implementing these into your strategy is probably a smart move.

Buyable Pins

Buyable Pins, as the name suggests, are those Pins that have a blue button found next to the red **Pin It** button. They allow Pinners to purchase the product they like, without having to leave Pinterest. How does it work? At this point, all businesses that are on *Shopify* have the opportunity to post Buyable

Pins, although they will surely become much more accessible in the near future.

Promoted Pins

Promoted Pins are, in a way, similar to Facebook promotions. You have to buy them in order to reach more followers. These Pins have the ability to increase the rate of engagement from 2 to 5 percent.

There is no minimum cost for these Pins, but the amount that you end up paying depends on your budget and the limit of spending that you set.

At this point, promoted pins are only available to business across the US, Canada, UK, France, Ireland, Australia, and New Zeeland.

Optimize and Engage for Success

Just as with any other social media platform, you will need to optimize your Pins in order to get your pins discovered and saved. It is one thing to make your pin amazing and visually appealing, but if you fail to optimize it for engagement, the beautiful imagery will not do you much good. Here are the ultimate optimization tips for Pinterest that your business should take advantage of:

Pin at the Best Times

If you ask https://www.hubspot.com/, they will tell you that the best time to post on Pinterest is on Saturdays, another platform will tell you that that's Sunday afternoon, but a good rule of a thumb is to save your Pinterest posts for the weeknights and weekends, as you have a lot more chance to be discovered at those times. However, if you want to be more specific, after a lot of research, I've pulled together enough comprehensive data to determine that these are the best times to post on Pinterest:

- Any day at 2-4 a.m., 2-4 p.m., and 8 p.m.-1 a.m.

- Fridays at 3 p.m.

- Saturday Mornings and Saturday Nights from 8 to 11 p.m.

This should work with any time zone, so give them a try and see if they work for your business.

Be Consistent

There are many posts that will suggest pinning up to 10 or even 15 times a day. Other say that once is the key, but the truth is, it is not about pinning a set number of times a day, but about Pinning consistently. If your business can benefit from sharing 20 Pins a day, then by all means, do it. Just keep in mind that if that's your goal, then you should stick to it and provide consistency to your audience. Be consistent so that your followers will know what to expect from your brand.

Make It Easy to be Pinned From

Your content – whether on your website, blog, or your phone app – should be easily Pinnable. If it's not clear to people where they should click in order to pin your content, they will not do it. It's as simple as that. Make sure to download the special widget   https://business.pinterest.com/en/pinterest-widget-builder#do_pin_it_button that will add a **'Pin It'** button next to your images, so that people can conveniently Pin from your site.

This actually increases pinning ten times, so do not skip on installing this button.

Pinterest's SEO

Having a decent SEO strategy is more than required, it is essential if you want to attract new Pinners and increase your Saves. When it comes to Pinterest searches, there are only 4 steps of good optimization:

1. Do thorough research on the keywords that are relevant for your business

2. Add those keywords (or keyword phrases) to the titles of your Pins

3. Incorporate the relevant keywords in the Pins' descriptions.

4. Add them to the file names of your Pin images.

For the millionth time, don't go in over your head. Keep in simple and don't use too many keywords. You don't want to be overly selling, but to sound human.

Comment!

It is needless to say but responding to the comments of your followers really goes the extra mile. It shows people that you care about them, that you value their opinion, and that you want to keep them informed and content. Make sure to respond to all of your followers' comments and do it within a day. There is no such thing as "stupid comment". Even if the comment doesn't require a response, such as "Love the color", you should always tell your audience that you value your opinion, at least with "Glad to hear that. Thank you for your feedback".

Commenting is a two-way street. Just like you want your followers to comment on your Pins, you should also leave comments on their boards too. Besides, this will only expose you to a wider audience as their followers will see your comment and your brand as well.

Leveraging Pinterest Marketing in 3 Steps

Even though Pinterest is a platform that is different than the other social media networks, Pinterest Marketing really doesn't require that different approach. When you think about it, it all boils down to just having a clear tactic that will collide with the set business goals you have. To wrap it up, here are the three steps to having a successful Pinterest Marketing campaign:

Step #1: Build Your Brand's Authority

It doesn't matter what you are trying to sell, one of the greatest ways in which you can use Pinterest for your marketing purposes, is to make people become aware of your brand. This is often forgotten as small businesses are usually preoccupied with driving more sales, but what they don't understand is that brand recognition actually results in having more customers.

For instance, if you are in the weight loss niche, you can create a Pinterest board that will promote your products and combine them with other popular weight-loss Pins. That's the beauty of Pinterest, really. Not having to create the entire content yourself but mixing and matching your content with some of the most popular saves on this platform.

Step #2: Grow Your Reach

Although there are many different ways in which you can use Pinterest to grow your reach, one of the most popular techniques is leveraging group boards. The secret here is to team up with some popular Pinners who already have pretty large audiences. By collaborating with them, you get to expose your brand to their audience. Why would they want to do that? Because that way they will provide more value to their loyal fan base.

Just keep in mind that, in order for this joint venture to be successful, you will have to find a partner who has similar interests in order to reach to the right target audience.

Step #3: Drive More Traffic

Without the right traffic, you will never make enough online sales, period. And in order to drive traffic to your website, blog, or even your sales page, you will have to provide your audience with content that is attracting as well as helpful enough to be shared. Pining great visuals is by far the best strategy for driving more traffic, so make sure to use all of the previously mentioned tips and offer your followers content that is inspiring and desirable.

Getting Started with Snapchat

When you think about Social Media Marketing, the first platform that comes to your mind is definitely not Snapchat. However, just because it is not up to par with Facebook, Twitter, and Instagram, it doesn't mean that trying to promote your brand on Snapchat is a wild-goose chase. Quite the opposite.

Snapchat is taking the social world by the storm. It is constantly improving and gaining more users, so missing out on the Snapchatting journey can really be a huge strike for your business. Besides, where the competition is still not that fierce, don't you think that you will be at a slight advantage?

Setting Up the Account

If you are seriously considering giving Snapchat a chance, have in mind that this platform is way different that the ones we've already covered in this book. Here, marketing your brand will not be about using CTAs and links and directing the users to a specific landing page where they can buy your product. Instead, it will be about sharing your brand's story through photos and videos. It may not be a direct way of promoting your products, but it will surely be a great way to spread awareness and tell people know what your business is all about. Here is why businesses choose Snapchat:

- To target a new audience. Snapchat is the go-to platform for teens and millennials and if they happen to be your target audience, then your place is definitely among them.

- Visual sharing. You don't have to brainstorm paragraphs of written content here. The only thing you need to type in is the caption. Everything is visual which is why this platform is so appealing for some businesses.

- Brief posts and stories. Snaps are a 10-second video or a photo. Sharing with your audience will be a pretty quick task, so

Snapchatting will not require a lot of your time and effort.

- It all happens in real time. You cannot upload content on Snapchat. It all happens in the spur of the moment.

- Snaps are stories that are deleted after 24 hours (which is mainly the inspiration behind Instagram Stories).

- It has more than 300 million active monthly users, and it is no doubt that introducing your brand on Snapchat will help you increase the brand recognition.

Snapchat is an app created for smartphones only. That means that you can only use Snapchat on your Android or iOS, since it is not available on your desktop or tablet. To set up your Snapchat account and get started, the first thing that you need to do is to download the app. Head to your App Store or the Google Play Store and download the Snapchat app. Then, follow these simple steps:

1. Open the app on your smartphone. Click on **'Sign Up'**.

2. Enter your name and hit **'Sign Up & Accept'**.

3. Next, enter your birthday to verify that you are old enough to be using this app.

4. Choose your username. It has to be at least 3-characters long. Use the name of your business or something that represents it. Tap **'Continue'**.

5. Enter your desired password and click on **'Continue'**.

6. Add your email address.

7. Next, you need to verify your account. Enter your mobile number and you will receive a verification code.

8. Enter the received verification code. Once the code is verified, click on **'Continue'**.

9. Decide whether you want the app to upload your contacts or not.

Now that you've created your account, you will be prompted to take a selfie and add it as a profile picture. After that, click on the white ghost icon in order to select a few photos that best represent your brand.

Snapchat is quite different than the other platforms. In order to know what you are doing, you should have knowledge of its lingo. Here are the most important Snapchat terms you should know of:

Snap – A 10-second video or a photo you take with Snapchat

Story – A photo (or a series) that will last for 24 hours before being deleted

Score – This is the number found below your profile photo and it represents the number of snaps you've viewed and shared.

Chat – Comments with your community

Memories – Published snaps that have a permanent life and cannot disappear after 24 hours (think Instagram Stories Highlights)

Lens – Special effects that are added to the photos

Filter – This is added to the photos in order to commemorate an event

Geofilter – A filter that is added for location-based events

Snapcode – A code (like a QR code) that is used to add friends with a simple button touch

Adding Followers

Taking photos and sharing them on Snapchat will be pointless if you don't have an audience to share your content with. Keep in mind that Snapchat doesn't have a public feed. Your snaps can be seen either by individuals or with everyone who follows your account.

Having a business account, it is of great importance that you add as many people that are relevant to your brand as possible. Seek out followers yourself, don't just wait for people to discover your brand's Snapchat and send you a request.

Use the 'Add Friend' Option – Click on the ghost icon and then tap **'Add Friends'**. You will then see different way in which you can add friends, as well as some recommendations for people you can follow.

Use the Snap Code – By using the snap code, you can easily add friends with a simple button touch. Make sure to encourage people on public events or whatever you get the chance in order to grow your following.

Taking Your Snaps

Congratulations! Your brand is an official Snapchat user. Now that your account is up and running, it is time to learn how to actually take the snaps and share content with your audience:

1. Set your phone so that it faces the subject. For instance, if you are trying to take a snap

of your newest product, face your camera away from you and facing the product.

2. Tap the round button to take a photo. To post a video, press this button and hold it for 10 seconds while filming.

3. Add comments to your snaps before you actually publish them:

   Click the T icon for typing text
   Click the pencil icon for writing or drawing text
   Click the sticky note to add a sticker – or the scissor icon if you want to create one yourself

4. Click on **'Sent to'**.

5. Decide whether you want to send it to an individual, share with your entire audience, or save it as a *memory.*

6. Finally, click on the **'Save'** button.

Sharing Your Brand's Story

Having your brand present on Snapchat is a great opportunity for increasing awareness. But Snapchat is not like the other social media platforms. Also, if you are a brand, you cannot exactly use Snapchat for posting selfies and sending personal messages as your audience will be uninterested. You have to find a way to present your brand, but without boring those followers who like the selfies and prefer using this platform over the other social media networks.

Here are some ways in which most brands use Snapchat to tell their story. Give these tips a try and craft your own, unique way to share your brand's story with your audience.

Product Launch – Snapchat can actually be the perfect platform for sharing snaps of your newest product to announce a big launch.

Home Tours – If you are in the real estate world, sharing photos or quick videos or available homes on Snapchat can be one great strategy for getting some more offers.

Live Updates – Since Snapchat happens in real time, it is perfect for sharing updates from a live event. Whether a seminar, rock concert, a football match, or a parade, reporting live can be a great way for your brand to attract more viewers.

Product Demo – Have a new product you want to promote? Show your audience how it works or reveal some other hacks that can be done by using it. Short videos are great for this purpose, so don't be afraid to hit the record button.

Behind-the-Scenes Update – IF your audience is impatient for your new line to hit the stores, let them know how hard you are working on it by showing a couple of behind-the-scenes photos. This can be done by showcasing the hard work of your employees or simply by giving a tour of a certain part of your business that your audience doesn't get to see.

Call to Action – Ok, you cannot use CTAs like with other social media platforms, but you can surely create some snaps that can encourage your followers to take an action, whether it is to sign up or go to an online (or physical) store and make a purchase.

Guest Introduction – Want to introduce your guest for your next Twitter Chat, podcast, or your YouTube show? Snapchat can help you make the announcement in a few visual snaps.

Coupons – Did you know that businesses actually use the doodle feature on Snapchat in order to share discounts and promotional codes? Why not give this a try and see how this works for your business?

Target Specific Users – Do you think that you have some followers that can benefit from purchasing your products or services the most? Why not approach them directly via private messages and make them an offer? For instance, if you are an owner of a massage studio and you notice a stay-at-home mom of 4, you can send a private message to

413

her admiring her patience and hard work, and offering her a huge discount for a massage treatment or even a free massage? This may not only make her a paying customer in the future, but she will most likely end up recommending your business to her circle of friends.

Engage!

While sharing snaps on Snapchat is a great way to increase brand recognition, gain more followers, and keep the ones you have informed and entertained, Snapchat is not a one-way street. Making sure to encourage engagement on Snapchat is just as interacting with your followers matter on the other social media platforms.

When you swipe the bottom of a user's snap, you will see that there is a *Send a Chat* where people can write down your comments. That means that on every snap you post, your followers have the opportunity to engage with the content and ask questions. And I am not only asking for the price of the newest products or asking if that silk shirt comes in different colors. I am talking about making sure that each of your snaps is thoughtful and created with the purpose to keep your audience engaged.

Here are some tips on encouraging interaction from your community, that most Snapchatting businesses use in order to increase the rate of engagement:

Share Content that Requires a Response – Although this is probably easier to achieve on other social media platforms, posting content that requires a response on Snapchat is indeed possible. But just because you have no clue on how to achieve this doesn't mean that you shouldn't do it. Have your whole team involved and let each of them share with you what makes them respond to content. Pull out the best thoughts together and come up with the best strategy that works for your brand.

Ask Open-Ended Questions – It is a bit more challenging, but asking questions on Snapchat is surely possible. Want to draw the attention of your users? Take a snap and press 'T' to type in the question. Just make sure that your questions deserve a bit more than a simple yes or no to keep the conversation alive.

Encourage to Respond with a Snap – Ok, let's be honest. Snapchat is a visual app and people go there to take snaps and look at other people's images. Your audience will be probably more interested in responding to you with a snap than with a text, so make sure to give them the opportunity.

Be Creative and Ask Different Responses – Let your followers respond with stickers, doodles or a special filter. Let them get even more creative and ask them to actually make their own filter.

Be Humorous – Keep in mind that your audience is on Snapchat for light-hearted and fun content. They are not looking for deep and meaningful conversation, so make sure to turn on your humorous side in your posts.

Create a Contest – People love challenges and competitions. By creating one, you will not only get your audience thrilled to participate, but you will also get to make the lucky winner a happy person. For instance, have a competition where your followers should use your brand name in a fun sentence, or take a funny snap with your product, or show you a snap of your product doing something that is not its main purpose. The point is for people to get engaged with your brand. Announce a huge reward for the funniest person. For instance, a special membership, a really generous discount on an expensive line, free products or services, etc. This can help you spread brand awareness, increase the engagement rate, and ultimately drive more sales.

Respond to Every Snap and Comment – Just like wit every other social media platform, responding to every question, snap, or feedback – whether positive or not – can have a great impact on your relationship with your audience. Respond in kind and let your followers know that you appreciate when someone takes the time to reach out.

Reward People Who Reach Out with Snaps – If you want to further motivate your audience to engage with your brand, you should be ready to give them something in return. This is especially important for small businesses who don't have an established fan base just yet. By rewarding your audience, you get to promote your brand, spread recognition, and keep your followers interested in what you are offering as well. Let your customers know that for every shared snap they will be getting a 10 or 20 percent discount on a certain product or service.

Snapchat may not seem like the go-to platform for marketing your brand, but it definitely has valuable marketing opportunities to offer. By taking on the challenge to promote your business in this unique way, you show your audience another side of you that they cannot see on, let's say, Twitter.

Conclusion

I'd like to thank you for taking the time to read this book. I hope that the tips and techniques discussed herein will help you boost your marketing skills and make you understand that promoting your brand on social media doesn't necessarily mean having a giant budget to spend on advertisements.

With the right knowledge under your belt, a healthy commitment, and your will to get your brand through all that social media noise, your business can grow successful and reap the returns from your promotional campaign in no time.

Now that you have all the steps you need in order to create a killer marketing strategy and slay your competitors, the next step is to simply start walking toward your goal. Appealing content and satisfied target audience are guaranteed!

www.ingramcontent.com/pod-product-compliance
Lightning Source LLC
Chambersburg PA
CBHW051749200326
41597CB00025B/4491